COTTAGE GARDENING
IN NEW ZEALAND

COTTAGE GARDENING
IN NEW ZEALAND

Christine Dann

with photographs by
Tony Wyber

First published in 1990 by Allen & Unwin New Zealand Limited in association with the Port Nicholson Press, Private Bag, Wellington, New Zealand.

Reprinted 1991 by Bridget Williams Books Limited, P.O. Box 9839, Wellington, New Zealand.

ISBN 0 04 614016 6

Drawings and layout by Tim Galloway
Typeset by Typocrafters Ltd, Auckland
Printed by Toppan Printing Co. Pty Ltd, Singapore

FRONTISPIECE:
The characteristic jumble and opulence of the old-style cottage garden. Roses, lilies and achilleas all vie for attention in this Nelson garden.
CHRISTINE DANN

CONTENTS

ACKNOWLEDGEMENTS

Cottage gardening is a co-operative form of gardening, and writing a book about cottage gardening is also a co-operative endeavour. I am enormously grateful to the dozens of people who freely gave me their time, the opportunity to view their gardens and their excellent advice. I would especially like to thank Tony Wyber who, in addition to providing the beautiful photographs for this book, also had the original idea for it, and kept pushing until it happened; Barbara, Michael and Michele Perkins whose Auckland nursery and gardening experience is the basis of the indispensable advice on cottage gardening in northern New Zealand given in Chapter 7; and Ian Duncalf, who commented on the plants listed in the appendices and advised on their suitability or otherwise for northern parts.

Other gardeners, growers and experts whom I would like to thank for their ideas and inspiration include John Adam, Gillian Blackmore, Sharon Brass, Peter Brass, Tiddy Brenton, Tom Brooking, Geoff Brunsden, Liz Brunsden, Bridget Canning, Charlie Challenger, Kathy Dover, Barbara Duncalf, Ian Duncalf, Olive Dunn, Gordon Evans, Jane Evans, Dawn Fleury, Margaret Galbraith, Peter Goodwin, Angela Gunn, Jan Holman, Grant Iles, Lois Isaacs, John Johnston, Helen Leach, Di Lucas, Helen McGibbon, Deirdre McKechnie, Sally Marshall, Pam Morrah, Sheila Neilson, Marise Newbery, Marilyn Newlove, Bob Osborn, Gilian Painter, Valerie Pendred, Lynda

The English tradition transposed to the New Zealand landscape. Here an Elizabethan-style cottage with its climbing roses and gravel paths has made a graceful transition from the old world to the new.

Pelargonium Butterfly Leaved 'Crystal Palace Gem'

Pinkney, Allan Portman, Faye Portman, Mary Rea, Deane Robertson, Malcolm Shearer, Terry Shuker, Geoff Speeden, Ash Spice, David Stanford, Johanna Stewart, Thelma Strongman, Alice Thrum, Alistair Turnbull, Margaret Unwin, John Wilson and Sue Witteman. If I have missed anyone's name in sorting through my piles of interview notes and correspondence, please forgive me and consider yourself thanked.

And where would any author venturing into the past be without the definitely overworked and doubtless underpaid staff of our museums? In Auckland, Wellington, Nelson, Christchurch and Dunedin I received every assistance, and I am duly grateful.

The table on p. 88 is reproduced by permission of Heinemann Reed, a division of Octopus Publishing Group (NZ) Ltd, from *Organic Gardening in New Zealand* by Richard Llewellyn Hudson.

Finally, a big thank you to my dear friends Maud Cahill, Kathryn Megson and Neville Peat, who visited gardens with me, took photographs to aid my memory, kept me company and were most encouraging while I researched and wrote this book.

Christine Dann

PHOTOGRAPHIC ACKNOWLEDGEMENTS

Gardening is something of a global pursuit and I've been given considerable assistance from numerous people all over the world in selecting material for this book. I've visited very many gardens in Great Britain, Sweden and Greece and have been shown every courtesy and been given endless assistance. I am truly indebted to all the gardeners who let me roam about their gardens to photograph their treasures and efforts. There are too many people to thank individually.

I would especially like to thank Dr Martin Sykes from The Biological Institute at Uppsala, Sweden, for his assistance and guidance. I'm indebted to the British National Trust for letting me photograph some of their gardens, and the British Cottage Garden Society for directing me to some of their members' gardens.

So many people have made time and resources available that there are too many to list. However, special thanks must go to Mr B. Jones at St Martins Geranium Nursery in Christchurch, and to Olaf John, Wellington, for kindly supplying photographs of native plants in Chapter 6. David Bromley in England showed me what plantsmanship was all about, and Brenda Mills made life much easier with her excellent secretarial skills.

I would also like to thank Mark Reeder, Director of the William Paca Garden, and J. Dean Norton, Horticulturist at Mt Vernon, USA, for their interest and support. Lastly, but I feel most importantly, I would like to thank Christine Dann for seizing upon the idea so enthusiastically, and all the Old Florists who left so much fine material for me to work with.

Tony Wyber

PREFACE

When people asked me what I was doing in 1989 I replied, 'I'm writing a book on cottage gardening.'

'Oh', they (usually) said, 'What is a cottage garden?'

This book is an attempt to answer that question within the New Zealand context. Most people who know the term 'cottage gardening' usually think of it as a style of gardening raised to a fine art form in nineteenth-century rural England, beautifully painted by artists such as Helen Allingham, and reduced to a cliché by being reproduced in one-dimensional form on a thousand chocolate boxes and biscuit tins. You know the sort of thing – a whitewashed cottage, often half-timbered, with a thatched roof, sits nestled in a drift of flowers. Roses climb over the trellised porch and peep in at the latticed windows, hollyhocks and delphiniums send their tall spires upwards to brush the edge of the thatch, cabbages and carrots proudly share beds with lavender and pinks, old fruit trees lean gnarled branches across the picket fence, a ginger tabby is sunning itself in a patch of catmint and a little girl in a shady bonnet is applying her miniature watering can to a patch of pansies . . .

Rich in produce and perfume, riotous in colour and variety, and undeniably romantic was the traditional English cottage garden. But is this tradition relevant or appropriate to twentieth-century New Zealand?

In this book I argue that it is, but that we must make changes in the tradition to make it fit our time and place. In doing so we may be departing from the letter of the style, but we will be truly honouring the spirit. A spirit of self-reliance, of caring for land and people, of cherishing the useful and the beautiful and growing them together. We need this spirit just as much today as we ever did, and I salute the cottage gardeners of New Zealand who keep this spirit alive.

A Note on Names

Some people find it hard to learn names – of plants or people. When you have just learnt to call our biggest native tree a kauri and that pretty flower a snapdragon you can be horrified to discover that the 'real' names of these plants are *Agathis australis* and *Antirrhinum majus*. Are these scientific names just a bit of unnecessary bother, or does knowing them really help us to be better gardeners? Sorry, but the answer is yes. If you know a person only by their nickname of 'Ginger' you won't be able to look them up in the phone book. Like people, plants have their 'nicknames' or common names, like rimu or daffodil, and they also have their full names. Their genus name (which is like a human surname) comes first, and their species name (like a human first name) comes second. Species in the same genus are related, like cousins in the same family. Take the campanulas, for instance. *Campanula medium* is the common annual usually nicknamed 'Canterbury bells', *Campanula persicifolia* is its tall relation, and *Campanula carpatica* a tiny cousin. Campanulas come in different sizes and colours, but all of them have flowers which make reference to the meaning of the word *campanula* – they look like bells.

If you know a little Latin and Greek (and if you know English you will be surprised how much Latin and Greek you know) you can have fun working out what the names mean. Often they are both more accurate and more romantic than some of the common names. They also make it much easier to identify and record plants, since unlike nicknames the scientific names apply to one plant and one plant *only*.

Scientific names likewise get around the problem of variation in common names from place to place (the early Scottish settlers in Otago were busy planting 'whins', while further north in Canterbury their English cousins were planting 'gorse'), and the fact that one common name can be applied to several quite different plants. The name 'valerian', for example, is applied to both the genuine herbal valerian, *Valerian officinalis*, which has very pale pink flowers, and to that cheerful deep pink or red weed which brightens Wellington banks in summer, the false or red-spur valerian, *Centranthus ruber*. Doctoring yourself with one rather than the other could have unpleasant results!

One final point – sometimes a species comes in several 'varieties' or 'cultivars'. These are plants which are not found in the wild but have been especially bred by plant breeders. The variety or cultivar name is usually given in inverted commas after the species name: for example, *Lavandula angustifolia* 'Hidcote Blue'. The cottage gardener must pay attention to this point, as a small garden does not have room to waste on inferior varieties. You should always aim for the best.

The Kiwi garden transformed into cultural heritage – Margaret Stoddart's painting of her family home at Diamond Harbour, 1913.
ROBERT McDOUGALL ART GALLERY

Chapter 1

COTTAGE INSPIRATION

The faint, acrid smell of smouldering leaves came in my open window all night, and there was still a tang of it in the sweet, crisp air when I woke before five o'clock the next morning. I was very tired, but there was yet another garden job to be done, one that could not wait another summer day. I had to pick the lavender, and it must be picked in the dawning, before the sun had stolen any of its sweetness.

The first quavering bird note floated across the garden in exquisite hesitancy. I lay very still and listened, entranced with the beauty of the morning. Out beyond the mauve and scarlet sweet peas that curled up over the windowsill of my sleeping porch I could see the sky, all soft, pastel tones, unlit by the fires of sunrise.

Lavender morn! – that was the very colour of the sky, the colour of the air, still misty with smoke. Not a breath of a wind to sway the flowers, not the faintest sound of voice or traffic – just the lavender sky and the scent of flowers, and the poignant-sweet song of a blackbird down in the orchard.

The lavender-blue of the sky was by now a lake, set in shores of silver; the little clouds that stretched away over the horizon like swallows in flight were caught suddenly in a rosy web of light; in a moment the lavender lake was swept into a golden crucible, and flames of glorious light went leaping up – up – into the sky.

With the birds singing in full chorus and long, golden arrows of the rising sun striking through the poppies, turning them into rosy chalices, piercing the green jungle darkness of the orchard, I wandered down the daisy paths, cutting the lavender. The scent of the sweet pile in my basket was exquisite. In it lay all the beauty and gladness of a garden, all the loveliness of spring and the gracious fulfilment of summer, all the lure and witchery of little winds, bird-song and the pageantry of beauty that is the dower of a garden.

Give it up? I laughed aloud. A white butterfly came darting down a sunbeam and fluttered round my basket. I watched it, entranced, held out my hand very gently, but the little white ship floated away again on a dancing wave of gold . . .[1]

The Indian pink (Dianthus chinensis) was much loved by Victorian gardeners. It is still available, and in this colour – stunning for a summer display.

In the heart of Auckland, in the depths of the Second World War, Elsie Morton kept cherishing her mother's cottage garden as her mother had once cherished family and garden alike. Laughing at her amateur bungles, and wryly entitling her account of her efforts *Gardening's Such Fun!*, Elsie Morton was acutely sensitive to the beauty and meaning of cottage gardening, as the passage quoted above confirms.

By 1850, six hundred years after the first cottage gardens were planted in England, cottage gardening was alive and flourishing 19,000 kilometres from its country of origin. After three centuries of changing and growing in Britain, developing better varieties of native plants and evaluating and naturalising new plants brought home by soldiers, sailors and merchants, the cottage garden itself was exported to each successive British colony established in temperate zones.

One hundred years before Elsie Morton rhapsodised about her urban cottage garden, the first New Zealand cottage gardens were receiving favourable comment. In December 1848 Howard and Heber Lakeman described their visit to Nelson thus:

In the vicinity of the town are a number of houses dotted about among the dark verdure, whose careful building, and gardens nicely fenced, with shrubs trained inside, and filled with roses, pinks, sweet williams, peas (and in fact every kind of flower), and young fruit trees, make no despicable imitation of an English house, and in six years will equal it.[2]

G. B. Earp, reporting on New Zealand four years later, thought that New Zealand gardens were well on the way to surpassing English gardens, remarking that:

no English garden, however expensively kept up, can for a moment vie with the beauty of a cottager's garden in New Zealand in the beauty of its shrubs, to say nothing of the vines, melons, Cape gooseberries, peaches, all English and many tropical fruits, which will grow anywhere in the greatest luxuriance.[3]

And Sarah Courage's apprehensive immigrant heart was gladdened by the sight of the cottages of Lyttelton, where she noted that:

the one-storied houses were objects of beauty; the verandas covered as they are with bright creeping plants; while high up on either side of the hills, gardens were laid out in square enclosures here and there, green and beautiful. Round the cottages the gardens were glowing with the gayest flowers.[4]

The nineteenth-century British immigrants were arriving at a time when cottage gardening was flourishing in Britain, and was finally being recognised as a desirable vernacular style, a subject for inspiration and imitation by educated gardeners. The great garden designer Gertrude Jekyll noted that:

Some of the most delightful of all gardens are the little strips in front of the roadside cottages. They have a simple and tender charm that one may look for in vain in gardens of greater pretension. And the old garden flowers seem to know that there they are seen at their best; for where else can one see such Wallflowers, or Double Daisies, or White Rose bushes; such clustering masses of perennial Peas, or such well-kept flowery edgings of Pink, or Thrift, or London Pride.[5]

Gertrude Jekyll held 'the firm belief that the purpose of a garden is to give happiness and repose of mind . . . and to give it through the representation of the best kind of pictorial beauty of flower and foliage that can be combined or invented.'[6] Simple combinations were often better than complicated ones, and Jekyll praised the cottage garden on this score too.

But cottage gardens were not only beautiful, they were also useful. The combination of beauty and utility is the essence of the cottage garden. Fruit,

vegetables and herbs are essential to the classic cottage garden, and many of the old-fashioned cottage flowers had traditional uses. Pinks, for example, were used for flavouring wine – hence their quaint nickname of 'sops-in-wine'. Lavender was utilised for scenting linen and baths, poppies for inducing sleep and flavouring bread, roses for pot-pourri, cowslips, elder-flowers and other blossoms for making wine, marigolds for flavouring and colouring stews, and so on. The middle-class Victorian garden, on the other hand, made a firm distinction between the ornamental and the necessary. Purely frivolous plants were cultivated assiduously and displayed ostentatiously by those with surplus income to proclaim; the mundane and modest members of the vegetable world were pushed out of sight.

Class distinctions among plants are anathema to the cottage gardener, and the tradition of combining beauty and utility struck firm roots in New Zealand. In the 17 March 1919 issue of the *New Zealand Fruitgrower* a head-line announced an article on 'Beauty and Utility in the Home Garden', and Mr H. G. Cutler of New Lynn proclaimed:

The combination of beauty and utility which should be the object of every home gardener, whether he lives in a cottage or a mansion, leaves plenty of scope for ingenuity and initiative, it inculcates a love of cleanliness, order, and the beauties of nature, and from the practical standpoint provides a ready means of meeting one of the greatest problems of the age, the cost of living . . . Every garden, large or small, should have its fruit, its flowers, and its vegetables.[7]

This picture shows what can be achieved in less than a year in Marlborough conditions.
CHRISTINE DANN

Throughout the nineteenth century male gardeners had provided plenty of sound written advice on *how* to grow a cottage garden, and they kept up this sterling work in the twentieth century. However, the reasons they gave on *why* cottage gardens were desirable were generally utilitarian and even moralistic, and it was twentieth-century women gardeners who provided the complete rationale for the cottage garden. Elsie Morton was an amateur speaking from the heart, but her views were seconded by professionals. Across the Tasman, Edna Walling had been designing Australian gardens for twenty years when she wrote in 1947:

Always a cottage garden is visualised as being one that is packed with flowers, not masses of separate species in rows and beds of 'exhibition strains' of this and that, but all kinds jumbled up together, the tall sheltering the low, and the fragrant justifying their presence even when their colour and form may not; a veritable patchwork of colour, a Liliputian fairy land of spires. Always there is a little pathway of stone or bricks, always there is lavender, and herbs, and rosemary and climbing roses wherever support may be found for them.

There is no formality, nothing stereotyped, not the slightest thing to recall the rather self-conscious gardens of the suburbs with the same proportion of lawn (never more than a week long) and the same well-trimmed hedge; for here in the cottage garden the picture develops by 'slip' and cutting, by root and seed, brought in a neighbour's basket and poked into some quickly stirred up patch of soil that happens to be unoccupied.[8]

Edna Walling took her cue from cottage gardens when designing larger gardens, creating natural, restful, prolifically planted places. Her more famous

When restoring gardens, look for flowers that are in keeping with those of the original period. This is one of the very early pansies (1847) that would be perfect for villa gardens.

contemporary in England, Vita Sackville-West, was also an enthusiast for the cottage garden style. Within her great garden at Sissinghurst, Kent, she planted thickly, always striving for the cottage effect of natural profusion. If she ever had to leave her own garden, she said,

and move into a bungalow on a housing estate, or into a council house, I should have no hesitation at all about ruffling the front garden into a wildly unsymmetrical mess and making it as near as possible into a cottage garden, which is probably the prettiest form of gardening ever achieved in this country in its small and unambitious way. I should plant only the best things in it, and only the best forms of the best things, by which I mean that everything should be choice and chosen.[9]

Most New Zealanders live in bungalows, and our two-storey state houses bear a startling resemblance to the two-storey weatherboard Kentish cottages shown on pages 67 and 125 of Edward Hyam's book *English Cottage Gardens*. We also have lots of lovely little cottages left in our inner cities and countryside. So we have the housing to suit the style, and an ideal climate. But do we have the will to continue the cottage tradition and transform it into a unique indigenous style? Why should we bother?

The answers are blossoming and greening all around us, and sometimes a busy gardener stretches her back, replaces her weeding fork with a pen, moves from the flower bed to the kitchen table, and tells us why. A gardening grandmother, Maire Graham, wrote to *Dittany* in 1987:

Come with me as I wander among the fragrant herbs that I love. They are scattered all over our garden in a most higgledy-piggledy fashion. Here, inside the front gate and leaning over the path is one of my lemon verbenas; it is just waiting for a leaf to be squeezed by anyone passing by. A small rosemary divides the path leading to the lavenders, eau-de-cologne mint and a small southernwood, while down the other side grow more lavenders and mints and here near the yew tree grow scented pelargoniums . . . The pleasure I get from my garden is greatest when I see my grandchildren enjoying the fragrant delights. One of those moments came when I noted Jasmin, then barely aged three, hand-in-hand with one of my friends, leaning over the lemon-scented geranium and saying 'Smell that, it's lovely.'[10]

The scent of grandmother's garden – what memories it evokes! The cottage garden may nourish the body, but it also feeds the heart. Beautiful and useful, cottage gardens may go in and out of fashion, but they never lose their relevance.

*Low-clipped box hedges and
central island beds give a
clear picture of an early
formula for the New
Zealand front garden. More
intense planting accords
better with modern tastes.*
NELSON PROVINCIAL MUSEUM

Chapter 2

THE COTTAGER'S LEGACY

In the nineteenth century New Zealand was colonised by a great gardening nation, and most (but not all) of our gardening styles and practices are derived from English traditions. These traditions were in themselves heavily influenced by England's role as a colonising power, but first Britain itself was conquered and colonised several times – with interesting horticultural results.

While it is possible that the first inhabitants of Britain grew fruit and vegetables as well as grains, and it is believed that the Celtic colonisers of the fifth and fourth centuries BC brought some plants with them from the continent of Europe, the first authenticated records of gardening in Britain date from the time of the Roman occupation (55 BC–AD 410). The Romans in Italy had developed a very formal style of pleasure gardening, with long straight walks, heavily clipped hedges, topiary, statues, fountains and other architectural rather than floral features. They brought this style to Britain, and it lasted only as long as they did.[1] Twelve centuries were to pass before grand formal styles were once more in vogue in Britain.

The Plant Inheritance

The Roman style did not last, but the plant material the Romans brought with them did. After 2,000 years of plant introductions, it is not always possible to tell whether some plants are truly native to Britain, and at what era others were introduced, but it is known that a few plants which are still popular in cottage gardens are genuine pre-Roman 'old Britons'.[2] They include those quintessentially English Christmas plants, the holly (*Ilex aquifolium*) and the ivy (*Hedera helix*). Native British fruits were the sloe, elderberry, damson and crab apple, and native vegetables included broad beans, beets and parsnips. Very few of the hundreds of herbs available to later gardeners were available to the pre-Roman Britons, but marjoram (*Origanum vulgare*), southernwood (*Artemisia abrotanum*), common valerian (*Valerian officinalis*), tansy (*Tanacetum vulgare*), sweet cicely (*Myrrhis odorata*), comfrey (*Symphytum officinale*), vervain (*Verbena officinalis*) and calamint (*Calaminta grandiflora*) are known to have existed in England that long ago.

A cottage classic.

There were also a few attractive flowers from pre-Roman times which have made the wilderness-to-cottage transition. These include the cornflower (*Centaurea cyanus*), meadowsweet (*Filipendula ulmaria*), sea pink (*Armeria maritima*), heartsease (*Viola tricolor*), common mullein (*Verbascum thapsus*), Jacob's ladder (*Polemonium caeruleum*) and the dramatic common teasel (*Dipsacus fullonum*).

With the wheat cultivated by the Celts came the cornfield wildflowers which later graced cottage gardens – the yarrow (*Achillea millefolium*), the corn marigold (*Chrysanthemum segetum*), the corn cockle (*Agrostemma githago*) and the field poppy (*Papaver rhoeas*). To this very basic plant stock the Romans are known to have added important food plants, including cultivated fruit trees such as walnut (*Juglans regia*), fig (*Ficus carica*), medlar (*Mespilus germanica*), mulberry (*Morus nigra*), sweet chestnut (*Castanea sativa*) and plum (*Prunus domestica*), and herbs such as fennel (*Foeniculum vulgare*), dill (*Anethum graveolens*) and coriander (*Coriandrum sativum*). They also brought flowers, of which the most important were roses and the opium poppy (*Papaver somniferum*). The little scarlet pimpernel (*Anagallis arvensis*) and the common mallow (*Malva sylvestris*) were Roman introductions, possibly along with the valuable edging plants rosemary and box. Two less lovely Roman introductions were the poisonous hemlock (*Conium macula-*

tum) and *Onopordum acanthium*, now known as Scotch thistle. Vegetables believed to have been introduced by the Romans include leeks, onions, garlic, globe artichoke, cabbage, turnip, cucumber, asparagus, radishes, lentils, peas and celery.

After the Roman troops withdrew from Britain and the country became prey to successive waves of invasion, gardening seems to have regressed to hotch-potch plantings. Minimum plantings of herbs and vegetables rather than pleasure gardening seem to have been the order of the day.[3]

The revival of organised gardening in tenth-century Britain occurred with the spread of monastic orders which existed within an atmosphere of relative security. Gardens were essential to feed the monks and nuns (who were dedicated to a largely vegetarian diet), to doctor their ailments and those of the lay people in their care, and to provide flowers for the decoration of churches and shrines for holy festivals. Plans of these monastic gardens show that they were carefully designed in all essential respects, with easy access to water and manure, and lots of small square or rectangular beds which were often raised and devoted to only one herb or vegetable.[4] (It is interesting to see modern vegetable growers advocating a return to this type of garden design for the domestic vegetable garden – but more on this later.) In addition to the purely productive garden there was often an enclosure intended to provide food for the spirit – a pleasant place which contained ornamental plants and which was conducive to meditation.

An indication of what was grown in the early monastic gardens can be found in the Glastonbury *Herbal*, written in Anglo-Saxon at the beginning of the tenth century. Fruit included apples, pears, peaches, medlars, plums and cherries, and grafting was practised. Wine was an authentic English beverage at this time: the Domesday Book of 1086 records forty vineyards.

The decorative monastic gardens had their lay parallel in the 'pleasaunce' of the castle – a safe enclosure where roses and other climbing plants scrambled over walls and frames which provided bowers for amorous dalliance. Or there might be an artificial meadow that was more flowers than grass (in the manner of medieval tapestries), providing a place for women to weave flower garlands.[5] The really attractive flower stock available to both monastery and castle was still limited. Daisies (*Bellis perennis*), cowslips (*Primula veris*), foxgloves (*Digitalis purpurea*) and Ragged Robin (*Lychnis floscuculi*) were more wild things which came in from the cold and were nurtured in gardens, but they were not as decorative as roses (still limited to a few species), lilies (three or four species, of which the most important was the Madonna lily, *Lilium candidum*), daffodils (*Narcissus* spp.), pinks (*Dianthus* spp.) and paeonies (*Paeonia officinalis* rather than the popular modern *Paeonia lactiflora*, which originates in China).

Other flowering plants which found a place in medieval British gardens were valued more for their contribution to medicine, perfumery and culinary flavouring than their floral beauty. The well-stocked monastery garden of the Middle Ages would contain forty to fifty different kinds of herbs and flowers, including borage (*Borago officinalis*), chamomile (*Chamaemelum nobile*), fennel (*Foeniculum vulgare*), mint (*Mentha spicata*), parsley (*Petroselinum crispum*), thyme (*Thymus serpyllum*), savory (*Satureja* spp.), saffron

An example of a contemporary English cottage garden designed by Stephen Crisp for the Stoke National Garden Festival, 1987. It contains a breathtaking 205 species!

(*Crocus sativus*), marjoram (*Origanum vulgare*), chicory (*Cichorium intybus*), wormwood (*Artemisia absinthum*), southernwood (*Artemisia abrotanum*), catnip (*Nepeta cataria*), black mustard (*Brassica nigra*), flax (*Linum perenne*), opium poppy (*Papaver somniferum*), comfrey (*Symphytum officinale*), valerian (*Valerian officinalis*), feverfew (*Chrysanthemum parthenium*), clary (*Salvia sclarea*), meadow sage (*Salvia pratensis*), woundwort (*Stachys sylvatica*), yellow water flag (*Iris pseudocorus*), nettle-leaved bellflower (*Campanula trachelium*), woad (*Isatis tinctoria*), rue (*Ruta graveolens*), scabious (*Knautia scabiosa*), monkshood (*Aconitum napellum*), madder (*Rubia tinctorum*), tansy (*Tanacetum vulgare*), coltsfoot (*Tussilago forfare*) and perhaps a dozen other herbs no longer well known today. The herb garden has always relied on form, foliage and aroma rather than brightness for its aesthetic appeal, and it is interesting that this appeal has persisted over eight or nine centuries, despite dramatic changes in taste and fashion in other areas of gardening. The clever herb gardener can thus have a garden which is relevant to today yet also timeless.

Today's vegetable gardeners, however, would not find it appropriate to copy their medieval English counterparts. Vegetable variety was much more limited than herb variety. Root crops were restricted to turnips, parsnips and beets. Beans were a popular crop, especially for vegetarian monks, but broad beans were the only kind available. The main members of the onion family (onions, garlic, leeks) were all grown, but were more useful to the wealthier folk who used them for flavouring meat dishes. Lettuce and spinach were grown for salads and boiled greens, but the predominant green vegetable, the one mentioned most often in gardening and cook books, was the cabbage. Not much variety there – and the home orchard was even worse.

The medieval English fruit fancier had to be fond of apples and pears, because little else was available. Apples were obviously a most practical fruit, since they could be stored and cooked as well as eaten straight from the tree, and by the late Middle Ages there were dozens of varieties available, along with some pear cultivars. Berry fruits, however, were still gathered wild, and stone fruits (cherries, plums and occasionally peaches) were grown for market rather than cottage consumption.

This was the extent of the plant material available to the first cottage gardeners. Who were these people?

The First Cottage Gardeners

Until the mid-fourteenth century most land in England was owned by the Crown, by feudal lords who owed allegiance to the Crown, or by the church. Independent freeholding by the common people was very rare. Agricultural workers (the bulk of the population) worked the land of the feudal lords or the church, in exchange for a percentage of the crop and the right to protection in times of war. These workers clustered in small hamlets or villages, with little productive land around their houses, and went out from the village each day to plough and sow and reap and mow, or to tend animals.

In 1349 the Black Death reached England. By 1350 between one third and one half of the total population had died, and this had a dramatic effect on both land usage and the viability of the feudal system itself. With labour at a premium, agricultural workers were in a better position to bargain for improved working and living conditions, eventually making tenancy agreements with the landowners and paying rent rather than giving feudal service. They were sometimes able to rent or buy land adjacent to their cottages, and thus produce solely for themselves.[6] This change would have been particularly congenial to the growing class of village tradespeople who were to become the main carriers of the cottage gardening tradition in the centuries to come. An urban class of small manufacturers and traders was also expanding at this time, and their town gardens were often cottage gardens in size and function, if not always in appearance or location.

The cottage garden had arrived, but it still had some way to go to reach the idyllic abundance celebrated by nineteenth-century artists.

The Evolution of the Cottage Garden

The first country cottage gardens were large (up to four acres) and were really self-sufficient little farms, which focused more on raising grain and animals than fruit and vegetables. It was only as gardens became smaller, decreasing from one acre in Elizabethan times through to a quarter acre by the early nineteenth century, that the pressure came on to develop horticultural skills which would still permit self-sufficiency. Busy cottagers who did not have the time or funds to landscape a large area could manage a display of ornamentals around the house, and they began to collect and grow a greater range of hardy flowering plants.

From the fifth century onwards the range of flowers available to the cottage gardener increased. Crusaders returning from the Near East are believed to have introduced the cottage favourites *Rosa gallica*, the Turk's cap lily (*Lilium martagon*) and the Maltese cross (*Lychnis chalcedonica*). Protestant refugees fleeing to England from Europe in the sixteenth century were a more important source of beautiful flowers and useful vegetables. By the close of the sixteenth century more cottage classics were firmly established, and were beginning to collect their romantic common names, such as love-in-a-mist (*Nigella sativum*). Nasturtiums (*Tropaeolum majus*) were ramping over mounds and through fences; the 'filthy weed' (*Nicotiana* spp. or tobacco) was discovered to have flowers which smelt far more sweetly than its burning leaves; the double windflower (*Anemone coronaria*) was brightening spring gardens, and creeping Jenny (*Lysimachia nummularia*) was trailing her little yellow flowers down walls and banks. Crown Imperials (*Fritillaria imperialis*) stood to attention every spring; soapwort's (*Saponaria officinalis*) lush green and gentle pink was decorative as well as useful for washing delicate clothing; petals of the pot marigold (*Calendula officinalis*) brightened salads, coloured stews and were a soothing ingredient in medicinal salves. Lavender cotton (*Santolina chamaecyparissus*) made a cheap and neat edging to cottage-garden herb beds and could be used as an insect repellent as well; the curious masterwort (*Astrantia major*) became a recherché cottage favourite; hyacinths (*Hyacinthus orientalis*) gave a perfumed promise of spring; lily of the valley (*Convallaria majus*) was a must in scented spring bouquets, and *Pulmonaria officinalis*, ill-named as lungwort owing to its supposed ability to cure lung diseases, began to collect a host of more descriptive and appropriate names such as 'Soldiers and Sailors', 'Hundreds and Thousands' and 'Boys and Girls'. Keeping these plants company were honesty (*Lunaria biennis*), rose campion (*Lychnis coronaria*), 'African' and 'French' marigolds (*Tagetes erecta* and *Tagetes patula*), birthwort (*Aristolochia macrophylla*), rosebay willowherb (*Epilobium angustifolium*), dog's tooth violets (*Erythronium dens-canis*), snowdrops (*Galanthus nivalis*) and snowflakes (*Leucojum vernum*).

The cottage garden was now well on the way to having its own special plant material. However, more treasures were yet to come. Botany as an exact science began to develop in the late sixteenth century, and was both an aid and an inspiration to the amateur plant collectors who appeared at this time. The sixteenth century was an Age of Exploration for the English, and gradually the value of collecting and studying plants from newly discovered lands became apparent. By the seventeenth century it was given the seal of royal approval, with King Charles II sending his chief gardener, John Tradescant Jnr, on special voyages to America to collect plants. Tradescant was a pioneer of plant collecting, which reached its peak in the late eighteenth and early nineteenth centuries.

The sixteenth century also saw the publication of the first illustrated gardening manuals in English. William Turner's *Herbal* of 1568 was a scientific work, which linked British and European plants, and John Gerard's famous

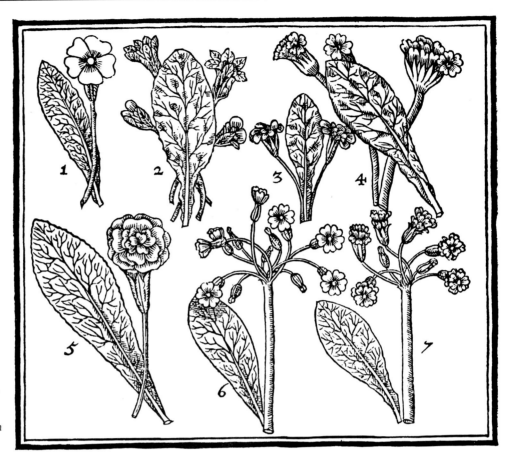

Some of the possibilities of cowslips and primroses presented by John Parkinson in Paradisi in Sole, *1629.*

Herbal of 1597, which ran to 1,400 foolscap pages and was illustrated with 1,800 woodcuts, gave advice on the cultivation and uses of hundreds of plants. Thirty-two years later John Parkinson's influential gardening book *Paradisi in Sole, Paradisi Terrestis* listed a greatly increased range of plants – for example seventy-eight varieties of daffodil compared to the twelve given by Gerard. The first British botanical garden was established at Oxford in 1621, and Britain was well on the way to overtaking Holland, Belgium and France as the premier plant-collecting and plant-breeding nation of Europe.

Most of the wonderful new additions to the gardener's store took a long time to enter cottage gardens. They were mainly grown in what must have been the rather jumbly gardens of wealthy enthusiasts. During the seventeenth and eighteenth centuries the gardening styles of rich and poor drew further and further apart. Francis Bacon's sensible sixteenth-century arguments in favour of gardens which focused on hardy plants, not artificial features, and which had something to show for every season, were ignored by the wealthier people he sought to influence, in favour of grand architectural styles of gardening. In the seventeenth century upper-class taste was influenced by French formalism, and imposing avenues, large parterres, mazes, fountains and other formal features were the order of the day. Only fine and large trees, clippable shrubs and choice (often tender) flowers were desired in such gardens.

During the eighteenth century there was a further shift in gardening taste among the wealthy, and the landscape garden, an English innovation, became sought after. Although it was more appropriate to English conditions

The inspiration which William Robinson placed before English gardeners: the cottage garden.

and made a greater contribution to English garden aesthetics than previous derivative styles, the landscape garden was almost diametrically opposed to cottage gardening. Seeking to create an Arcadian illusion, it required that productive agriculture and horticulture be banished from sight, with only glimpses of pastoral farming and forestry admissible. Human figures in the landscape were shepherds playing pipes on grassy knolls, not labourers sticking spades into vegetable beds. Landscape garden designers focused on the correct siting of noble trees and flowering shrubs, and gave little thought to the content and placement of vegetable and flower gardens. They offered little in the way of inspiration and support for the traditions of the cottagers.

This was not a problem, since economic sense dictated that cottage gardeners stick with hardy perennial flowers and a slowly widening range of vegetables and fruit. The big estates had no time for such sweet but modest flowers as stock (*Matthiola incana*), columbine (*Aquilegia vulgaris*), meadow cranesbill (*Geranium pratense*), everlasting pea (*Lathyrus latifolius*), forget-me-not (*Myosotis sylvestris*), wallflower (*Cheiranthus cheiri*), snow-in-summer (*Cerastium tomentosum*), pasque flower (*Pulsatilla vulgaris*), evening primrose

(*Oenethera biennis*), Star of Bethlehem (*Ornithogalum nutans*) and red valerian (*Centranthus ruber*) which were appropriate to the increasingly small scale of the cottage garden during the seventeenth and eighteenth centuries. By the end of the period most cottage gardens were less than an acre in size, and in the early nineteenth century various social reformers with an interest in the countryside began to advocate one rood (a quarter of an acre) as the optimum size for self-sufficiency in fruit and vegetables for a cottage family.

At this time cottage gardening entered a new phase.[7] Its contribution to the national economy was recognised, with home production making a significant contribution to the standard of living of cottagers. Conscientious (or canny) landowners made improvements to the 'tied' (tenanted) cottages on their estates and encouraged cottage gardening. Exploitative or lazy landowners developed their own personal homes and gardens at the expense of their workers. The originators of cottage gardening – agricultural labourers – found it harder and harder to maintain their homes and gardens as the economy shifted from agricultural to industrial production.

But by then a new class of people was taking an interest in cottage gardening, not as an attractive compromise with necessity, but as an aesthetic style in its own right. People who could afford city villas were turning instead to country cottages, and were interested in maintaining the types of plants and styles of planting developed by the original cottagers. There was also a growing revulsion of taste against the middle-class Victorian garden with its specimen shrubs dotted in an expanse of lawn, its multiple geometric flower beds plastered with exceedingly bright dwarf plants, its ornate glasshouses and gazebos, its grandiose statuary and geometric topiary, its excess of formal walks and driveways and its other ponderous, unnatural features.

Thus cottage gardening came to be re-interpreted. No longer a naive style born of necessity, it was studied and developed as a conscious gardening style, and its principles were applied to some of the great English gardens of the late nineteenth and early twentieth centuries.

As a definite style, rather than a naive adaptation to circumstances, cottage gardening remains relevant to contemporary gardeners. As a British tradition, it has been carried around the globe. Perhaps New Zealand, which matches Britain most closely for climate, is the best place in which to look for changes in the cottage garden which are dictated by new plant material and new ways of living.

The flowers came first, then the fruit and vegetables, to enhance this brand new 1880s cottage.

Chapter 3

COLONIAL COTTAGERS

My second New Zealand cottage garden, which flourished amazingly as I wrote this book, was based on two sections which were surveyed in 'the village of Rothesay' (now the suburb of Ravensbourne) in the 1870s. Together the two titles cover one quarter of an acre – the perfect size for a Kiwi cottage garden.

Inscribed on hundreds of thousands of land deeds, many of them more than a century old, and immortalised in the title of a book, *The Half-gallon Quarter-acre Pavlova Paradise* by Austin Mitchell (1972), the desirability of the quarter-acre section is so ingrained in Kiwi consciousness that no one questions why or how it came to assert a dominant influence over urban landholding. Pending a thorough historical investigation of the subject, I can only offer a few hints on how the size and style of the cottage garden were transported from Great Britain and evolved in their own characteristic ways in New Zealand.

In *The Cottage Garden*, a history of English cottage gardens, Anne Scott-James shows that there was debate among landlords and social improvers in the late eighteenth and early nineteenth centuries about the desirable size for the cottage garden. Some experts favoured a quarter acre, while others thought that an eighth of an acre was sufficient. The smaller size presumed a very small crop of potatoes, no standard fruit trees and the creative use of wild food.[1] It was obviously not enough for self-sufficiency in New Zealand pioneer conditions: here self-reliance was for real. Not only were there no handy hedgerows for foraging or markets for trading if one's garden failed, there was also no tradition of tenants' 'perks' which cottagers in Great Britain had come to rely on. There the majority of cottagers were farm labourers, who often rented their cottage from their employer, and the perks they might expect included free straw for a pig, pigs at cheap prices, cheap wheat, free kindling and gifts of food and money at Christmas.

However, there is also evidence that during the nineteenth century these perks began to be withdrawn, and cottage gardens in Great Britain became smaller. Wages for farm work were also cut, rendering labouring cottagers so hard pressed that they began to form county-based agricultural labourers' unions to defend and restore their rights. These unions had a unique solution to the problem of the over-supply of their labour forcing down wages – emigration. Union representatives travelled to New Zealand to see if conditions were as good as the authorities said they were, and were sufficiently impressed to advocate emigration for British farm labourers. In *The Farthest Promised Land* Rollo Arnold outlines the role the British agricultural unions played in the settlement of New Zealand by labouring people in the 1870s. These immigrants came mainly from the southern counties of England, where cottage gardening was generally agreed to be at its best.[2]

Thus we know that 'real' cottagers, heirs to the 'real' cottage garden tradition of England, came to New Zealand. However, we know frustratingly little about what they did when they got here. Photographic evidence of cottage gardening in New Zealand can be found in museum archives, but it is impressionistic, and provides no clear picture of how typical or widespread the practice was. Nevertheless, such impressions do allow us glimpses of what some people were doing as part of the broader canvas.

It is pleasant to imagine that there were hundreds of children like ten-year-old Helena Barker, observing the establishment of cottage gardens in a new land, though few of them wrote as she did about her parents' garden in Feilding in 1876:

Our section is all under cultivation now, that is the one acre. We have apples, plums, black currant bushes, and strawberries planted, and the remaining part will be potatoes and corn, and mother is cultivating a small flower garden in front. Father has a nice black horse, and we have killed one little pig about 10 stone . . .[3]

Pioneer Plants

Although it is difficult to find out about patterns of domestic land use, it is comparatively easy to find out what plants were grown. Pakeha settlers wrote letters, kept diaries, issued catalogues, founded horticultural societies, entered horticultural shows, and wrote books and newspaper articles on plants and gardens. From these it is possible to trace the entry of the traditional English cottage garden plant stock to New Zealand and to notice how quickly it was supplemented or supplanted by alternatives which did better in New Zealand conditions.

Helen Leach documents one of the first Pakeha gardens in New Zealand in *1,000 Years of Gardening in New Zealand* as follows:

Within a few months of these plantings, a plan was drawn up for setting out the grounds around the Kerikeri Mission (now known as the Kemp House). The vegetables were to be divided among a number of rectangular beds of four basic sizes, with paths between them in typical English kitchen-garden style. One bed was devoted to hops and, over all, nearly 3,000 square metres were set aside for fruit and vegetables. We know exactly what these were from Marsden's list of 1821–22: hops, turnips, carrots, radishes, cabbages, potatoes, lettuce, red beet, broccoli, endive, asparagus, cresses, onions, shallots, celery, rock and watermelons, pumpkins, cucumbers, parsley, grapes, strawberries, raspberries, oranges, lemons, apples, pears, peaches, apricots, quinces, plums and almonds. Peppermint and spearmint, sage, lavender, rosemary and rue seem to have been the only herbs, while the flowers appear to have been confined to marigolds, lilies, roses, pinks and sweet william . . .

An aura of tranquillity pervades this lush garden in Nile Street, Nelson.
NELSON PROVINCIAL MUSEUM

This, then, was basically an English collection of vegetables and fruits if we include items such as watermelons, oranges and lemons, formerly grown under glass. Both maize and sweet potatoes, the important Maori crops, are absent from the list.[4]

By the time Charles Darwin visited Northland in 1835 the missionaries' houses were sporting a variety of cottagey flowers, such as roses, honeysuckles, jasmine, stocks and sweet brier. They were also freely growing fruit which required special care in England, such as figs, olives, grapes, melons, loquats and citrus fruit.[5]

During the ensuing thirty years English-style gardens were established for the first time all over New Zealand. Sarah Greenwood wrote to her English relations from Motueka in November 1844:

We have now in the garden, Potatoes, cabbages of various kinds, beans (broad and kidney), lettuces, onions, turnips, carrots, vegetable marrows, Maori melons, spinach, rhubarb, sea kale, pot herbs, beetroot, raspberries, strawberries, plum trees, almond, damsons, gages (green and yellow), peach and nectarine, apple and pear trees, so you see we shall shortly be well supplied.[6]

Charlotte Godley too was keen on gardening, and wrote eagerly of her efforts to the folks back home. A garden had already been established at the house her family rented in Wellington in 1850, and in April of that year she wrote:

The garden is really very pretty, only a little out of order; with sweet brier, honeysuckle, clove pinks and white moss roses, and other real English plants, scarcely yet out of flower, and overrun with fuchsias, which make hedges, almost. There is some kitchen garden too, so that we have been eating our own cabbages, horse radish, and lettuce, and there are lots of watercresses in a stream close by.[7]

More details were given in August, as follows:

It is very good of Aunt Charlotte to think of us and our seeds; those she has sent will be most valuable; also the idea for a speculation in mulberry trees, but I am not sure that the plants are to be had here. It is, I suppose, rather characteristic, in an *English* colony, that the gardens here are full of English plants and trees. We have in this garden (e.g.) quantities of fuchsias, roses (which don't seem to do very well), sweetbrier, pinks, honeysuckle, daffodils just now coming into flower, and so on and, besides the acacias very few native things except one, very like an evergreen privet, and a low bush, like yew but covered with berries. There are grapes too, figs, nut bushes, and one oak, about 8 feet high.[8]

By September the violets were out – large doubles and white and blue singles – and there were also wallflowers and stocks. By November Charlotte Godley was noticing that New Zealand gardens behaved differently from English ones: 'The gardens are all looking lovely, and the things grow too quickly. I mean that vegetables, for instance, have run to seed before you know where you are.' However, the good side of early maturity was also apparent: some strawberries and cherries were already ripe, and 'tomorrow there is to be a flower show'.[9]

The following year the Godleys moved to Lyttelton. They sent their seeds ahead of them, and discovered that the ones planted at the Deans brothers' farm at Riccarton (now a suburb of Christchurch) came up, whereas those planted at Lyttelton failed. This led Charlotte to observe what did do well in Lyttelton: 'Those settlers who came out in ships, touching at the Cape [of Good Hope], generally brought supplies of flowers and shrubs from there, and they all do uncommonly well, and even bear the wind pretty well, which roses do not.'[10]

When Samuel Butler sailed into Lyttelton in 1860, he was more interested in the distinctive native vegetation, such as flax. But by 1861 he had established what may have been the highest cottage garden (at 1,700 metres) in New Zealand at that time. This was sited at Mesopotamia, his high-country station beside the Rangitata River. He described its September 1861 state to his aunt:

. . . my garden, which is now beautiful in a culinary point of view, green peas coming into blossom, potatoes well up, asparagus bed made and planted . . . I have a few rose trees, carnations and narcissus, a daffodil, some poppies, stocks, sweet williams, wallflower and larkspur – all in two little beds on either side [of] the gate. The rest is chiefly potatoes and other vegetables. I have three little pear trees, three peach trees, four plum trees and four cherry trees.[11]

The first Pakeha settlers brought their seeds, bulbs and cuttings with them, and wasted no time in planting them. As early as 1844, however, commer-

cial nurseries had been set up to cater for the increasing demand for healthy plants in great variety. Neil McVicar established the 'Neilann Nursery' in Nelson's Trafalgar Street South in 1844, and by 1850 he was advertising for sale:

Apples, 30 named varieties	£6 per 100
Plums and cherries	
Moorpark apricots	2/- ea.
Pears, assorted varieties	2/- & 2/6 ea.
Grape vines, choice varieties	1/- ea.
Red, black and white currants	3/- per doz.
Assorted gooseberries	4/- per doz.
Scotch firs, stone pines, Pinus pinaster	4/10/- per 100
Black & white Italian poplars	1/-
English lilac	1/-
Syringa	2/- ea.
Roses in variety	1/- ea.[12]

In 1848 William Hale was offering Nelsonians 'Crocuses, 12/- per 100, £5 per 1000, Turban ranunculus, 16/- per 100, £5 per 1000, Lily of the Valley crowns, pinks and picotees, all moderately priced.' Liliums were priced from 7/6 to 25/- per bulb. By 1853 Hale had 10,000 fruit and other trees for sale, among them apricots, peaches, pears, plums, nectarines, filbert nuts, currants, gooseberries, grapevines, ash, elm, oak, poplar, holly, laurel and laurustinus.[13]

In the 1860s nurseries and seed suppliers began to issue catalogues of their wares, and these make stunning reading, both for the variety and the quantity of plants on offer. Tucked among the more exotic items in the 1863 catalogue of Auckland's premier nineteenth-century nurseryman, David

Hay, are the cottage classics anemone, snapdragon, wallflower, hollyhock, pansy, polyanthus, violet, narcissus, delphinium, sweet William, poppy, nasturtium and marigold. While some of the nursery offerings were way beyond cottage budgets, thrifty cottagers who knew how to propagate plants would have had no difficulty in getting hold of the full range of English traditional plants. They also had the opportunity to buy and grow a far greater variety of fruit and vegetable seeds and plants than is easily obtainable today.

From the 1870s onwards nurseries and seed merchants routinely offered *hundreds* of varieties of the popular fruits, such as apples and pears, and a choice of nuts, figs, citrus, mulberries and other less common fruits which would make today's members of the New Zealand Tree Crops Association sigh with envy. All reputable seed sellers also offered at least fifteen to twenty varieties of the most common vegetables (potatoes, peas, cabbage), and anyone who thinks that capsicums, aubergines, salsify, endive, globe artichokes, okra and shallots are trendy vegetables which owe their appearance on New Zealand dining tables to the yuppie explosion of the 1980s will be chagrined to read catalogues like that of Law, Somner and Co. of Mosgiel and East Taieri from 1881. These wholesale and retail seed merchants and nurserymen sold all these vegetable seeds, along with *twenty-seven* varieties of rock melon seed. Of course we don't know how many gardeners deviated from the traditional English cottage repertoire to grow such vegetables, but at least one conservative Scotsman gardening in Christchurch at the turn of the century did. Jean Lawrence describes her grandfather as growing 'all the usual vegetables – the full range', but also taking 'pride in exotic vegetables as well: curlykale and kohl rabi, salsify and globe artichoke, celeriac and kumaras, even mushrooms.'[14]

The distinctive New Zealand cottage garden had begun to grow.

The Pioneer Experience

It was hard work getting started. Francis Pillans settled at Inch Clutha in January 1850, the second Pakeha settler in South Otago. He had a lot to learn about gardening in Otago conditions. He sowed his early potatoes on 30 July, and then dug a few up on 10 September to see how they were getting on. He noted in his diary that they had 'laid in the ground a month and ten days without the slightest use' as they had only begun to 'shew symptom of springing'.

A few days later he sowed vegetable seeds and fifteen different kinds of flower seeds. The peas and beans were up by October, but the spuds were still sulking in the ground. On 11 October Pillans sowed a variety of tree seeds, and on 15 October he noted in his diary: 'I should say noone in all New Zealand has such a large fine collection of seeds in the ground as we have but it remains to be seen what will come of it.'[15] Unfortunately, and to our continuing cost, only the 'whins' (gorse) were a roaring success.

Although Pillans was a novice gardener and farmer he was an educated man who had seen a lot of the world, and his cottage garden included hot frames where he grew cucumbers and melons as well as tree seeds. Cucumbers in the open ground did poorly, as did most of the vegetables planted in the summer of 1850, for December was very cold, with snow and sleet.

However, on Christmas day Pillans was pleased to record: 'We gave them a fair feed of all things, having for the first time broken in upon our vegetable garden. We were fortunate enough therefore to sport a dish of peas, some turnips and little green leeks.'[16]

The following spring Pillans was still having trouble getting foreign tree seeds to grow, though native tree seeds were more rewarding, and in November 1851 he was experimenting with planting potatoes in 'Maori heaps' to compare the results with English methods. Although his was a bachelor establishment, Pillans did not neglect flowers, and he created a garden in front of his house which included geraniums, hollyhocks, pinks, carnations and calceolarias.[17]

This sort of trial-and-error gardening was going on all over New Zealand in the 1850s and 1860s, and some people were obviously succeeding. Dr James Menzies described the cottages in the Hutt Valley in January 1854 as follows:

the road is lined by neat, wooden cottages, on the clearings, having little flower gardens nicely laid out in front, the verandahs generally covered with roses, woodbine, convolvulus and other climbing plants, the latter and clematis being common in the forest.[18]

A new settler with a strong interest in horticulture was Robert Dawber, from Lincolnshire, who visited Wellington and Nelson in 1869 before deciding that Akaroa was the ideal place for his gardening and fruit growing. In Nelson he was especially interested in honey production: 'Last evening we went into a cottager's garden who has more than forty boxes of bees; he has glass tops so as to take the honey without destroying the bees. In a bad year he says he takes 100lbs, in a good one 300lbs, and sells it at 1/-. per lb.'[19] Dawber was obviously impressed by these yields and the price, and went on

23

Gold laced polyanthus – the Victorian version. Plants of this quality can still be found.

to take more notes on beekeeping techniques. He also noted that scarlet passionflowers, common passionflowers and a pomegranate tree were flowering in Nelson, and sampled some of the home-made delicacies – gooseberry preserve, home-made cheese, and cherry wine.

Down in Akaroa the German and French settlers were also making fruit wines and even peach cider. Dawber visited a number of settlers, inquiring about land for sale, and noted of two German settlers that: 'They take great pains with their garden, and their orchard trees and garden produce are excellent.'[20] That Akaroa horticultural standards were generally high can be seen from Dawber's account of the Horticultural Show held on 3 March 1869:

Peaches three inches across, eleven inches round – Red Percy, White Percy. Splendid collection of fruit in large basket consisting of apples, peaches, plums, walnuts, small nuts, grapes, nectarines, almonds, pears, currants, quinces, figs. Peaches the largest I ever saw. Good nectarines, very large baking apples, Keswick Codlings and various other sorts. Ribston Pippins, golden Pippins &c, Magnum Bonum plums, figs, red currants, cherries, brambles, pears. The flowers were nothing to boast of except some fine Lilies. The vegetables were good, potatoes, carrots, kidney beans, vegetable marrows, parsnips, pumpkin, celery, cabbage, cucumbers, tomatoes &c, cheese, butter, honey, lettuce, onions. There is much fruit sent by steamers from Akaroa to Dunedin &c, also quantities of cheese.[21]

Soon Dawber was planting his own garden and orchard, on a property which, he'd been told, had on it the first grapevine and olive tree planted at Akaroa. They were soon joined by all the usual fruit trees in great quantity (Dawber planted forty-nine peach trees and fifty-two plum trees) and also some less common fruits – quince, fig, medlar, mulberry, sweet chestnut, almond. Dawber also began a flower garden, and in July 1869 transplanted young shrubs from the bush and put them in the flower beds.

Further evidence that nineteenth-century New Zealand was a hotbed of horticultural development and experimentation for cottagers as well as the upper classes comes from the schedule of the Auckland Gardeners Horticultural Society Autumn Show of 1887. This society was governed by a committee of 'twelve Gardeners [presumably professionals?] three Amateurs [middle-class or upper-class amateurs?], two Cottagers [working-class amateurs?], a Treasurer, two Auditors, and a Secretary'. The show had classes for gardeners, amateurs and cottagers, with cottagers being expected to show a smaller range of flowers and vegetables than the other classes. The schedule (the only one of its kind to reach the Auckland archives) provides a tantalising peep at the organisation of late nineteenth-century New Zealand, with plants and people both confined to classes.

Was everything in the Victorian New Zealand garden as tight and trim as the above impressions suggest? We know that the new colony did not work out quite the way its British planners intended it to, and this seems to hold true for gardening as well. Not everyone who immigrated knew much or cared much about gardening, and quite a number came from backgrounds where gardening was limited to the utilitarian essentials. Mrs McClinton of Canterbury, recalling her Aberdeenshire childhood, remembers that at her grandmother's place, 'There was not a great variety of flowers, nor yet a great

Framing cloud-like drifts of flowers, a curving path and wrought-iron gate add charm to this Nelson garden.
CHRISTINE DANN

number of them.'[22] This is the only mention of flowers in Mrs McClinton's extensive memoir of her pioneering days, and undoubtedly she was not the only immigrant with no interest in the subject.

However, many emigrants found that they were required to take a greater interest in gardening than they had back home, for reasons of sheer survival. Thus twelve years after the signing of the Treaty of Waitangi the first publication designed to facilitate gardening in the new colony appeared. This was the 'Gardening Calendar' contained in the *New Zealand Church Almanac*. Pioneer Christchurch nurseryman William Wilson also included a 'New Zealand Garden Calendar for all the year round' in the 1853 edition of the *Southern Provinces Almanac*, and this was reprinted every year until it was published between separate covers in 1878. Calendars were obviously important to immigrant gardeners from the northern hemisphere, who had to adjust to 'upside-down' sowing and harvesting times.

Seven other books containing gardening advice were published in New Zealand in the nineteenth century. The advice they gave was utilitarian, and expressed in utilitarian ways. Only H. J. Hawkins, writing on 'The Flower Garden' in Chapman's *Settlers' Handbook to the Farm and Garden* (1873) chose to philosophise about gardening, with what seems today like an excess of Victorian sentiment:

25

*With vegetables and flowers
all jumbled up together,
freshly planted fruit trees
will reinforce the obviously
utilitarian nature of this
garden in Richmond, Nelson.*
NELSON PROVINCIAL MUSEUM

Flowers have in all ages been cultivated by persons of leisure and taste, for the beauty and variety of their forms, colours and fragrance. While generally healthy and exhilarating, from its being pursued in the open air, flower culture is justly reckoned a pure and harmless recreation, which, by leading to the tranquil contemplation of natural beauty, and diverting the mind from gross worldly occupations, has a positively moral, and therefore highly beneficial tendency. It often serves to awaken in previously listless minds a spirit of inquiry respecting the great phenomena of nature and the laws of vitality, which so vividly exemplify the wisdom, and power, and goodness of the Creator. It is therefore available as a useful auxiliary of education, as a stepping stone to science; and as a means of elevating the moral character of a people, and their religious emotions.[23]

We get a hint that by the late nineteenth century all was not rosy in the New Zealand garden. Maybe it was the prevalence of the Hawkins attitude which was repulsive to working-class gardeners. Or maybe the rapid establishment of market gardens in the centres of the new cities quickly undermined horti-cultural self-reliance in urban dwellers. Perhaps later waves of immigrants were simply not keen on gardening. Alarm about the health of New Zealand gardening was expressed in the first edition of Michael Murphy's *Handbook of Gardening for New Zealand* (1885), which noted in the preface that: 'It is, unfortunately, a notable fact that vegetable growing is much neglected by the majority of small farmers. Cheap bread and cheap meat, with an abundance of potatoes, seem to satisfy most of those engaged in rural pursuits.' Murphy pointed out that a diet consisting mainly of animal food is not conducive to good health, particularly in children, and that vegetables purify the blood, and then went on to state: 'One quarter of an acre, well managed, would provide a large family all the year round with an ample supply of wholesome vegetables.'[24]

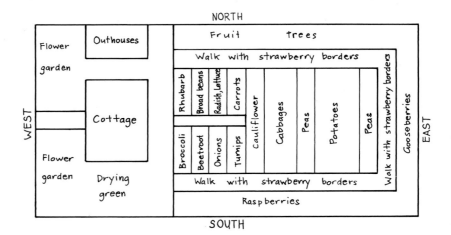

We don't know how widespread this failure to garden was, but can only hope that other provinces presented a better picture than the Waikato did to an anonymous observer who wrote in *Bond's Waikato Almanac* of 1892:

I have often experienced much surprise, when travelling about the Waikato district, at the great want that exists of small, well-kept gardens. This is not alone observed about the labourers' cottages, but also about many extensive farms as well, a small well-kept garden attached to either being the exception. Often when noticing a cottage garden with the grass run to weeds, and containing only a few stunted trees, with broken branches, I thought what a different picture it might be made with a little care and attention; besides the additional income it might be made to yield to its occupier.[25]

The writer then went on to give advice on the desirable content and layout of the cottage garden, including vegetables, fruit and flowers. The design suggested (above) is dominated by straight lines and rigid role divisions. There is a small area of flowers for the young girls to tend at the front of the cottage ('as there are very few of them who do not enjoy the fragrance and beauty of flowers, whether growing in the garden, or as nosegays in the hand, or bouquets as ornaments for their rooms') and a piece of lawn at the side of the house for a drying green or play space. This is on the *opposite* side of the section to the outhouse which would have contained the copper and wash tubs. (Since women's work is free why make it easier?) A large area at the back is devoted solely to fruit and vegetables in rows and rectangles, to be worked by the husband in his spare time and any boys, 'from ten to fifteen years of age, now often idling about, [who] might learn to do a lot of the work and find a pleasure in doing it'.

Was it the economic depression of the 1880s and 1890s which inhibited cottage gardening, or the mental depression induced by contemplating designs such as this?

Twentieth-century Trends

Such a functional but tedious style seemed to become synonymous with New Zealand cottage gardening in the early twentieth century. Flowers, vegetables and fruit trees no longer cohabited all around the house, but were allocated separate spheres and separate carers. Mixed plantings of herbaceous perennials gave way to rows of annuals; roses came down off the walls

Old-fashioned roses, 'Leda' and 'Debutante', scramble over a rustic archway in this Port Chalmers garden.

where they sprawled at ease and stood up straight in rows in front of the house; flowers were banished from the vegetable garden, and the front lawn continued its climb to archetypal significance.

In another tantalising peep through the historical curtain we are vouchsafed a view of the winner and runner-up gardens in the New Lynn Horticultural Society cottage garden competition of 1919, photographed for *The New Zealand Fruit Grower*. The winner had a typical weatherboard Kiwi cottage, a little box of a house with a verandah and an iron roof. It was partially obscured by wide borders of classic cottage perennials growing riotously on either side of a grass path which led to the verandah. The grass was a bit tatty, the beds were packed with clumps rather than drifts, more trees were needed to improve the scale of the design – but overall the flowers looked so lavish and healthy that this imitation of the English-style cottage garden still vindicated the style.

The runner-up, on the other hand, had a front garden which was much more like the New Zealand twentieth-century stereotype. The house was a brick and concrete bungalow, the paths were gravel or concrete, the small front lawn was divided into two halves, one with a round bed in the centre and one with a square bed, both beds containing one rose bush in the middle and an edging of sparsely planted, low-growing annuals. Everything was very neat and probably bright; riotous, lavish, varied and romantic it was not.[26]

Save space, enhance your garden, and provide a strong feature by espaliering fruit trees on warm walls.

Obviously the judges of this competition (and our Waikato critic) based their definition of 'cottage garden' on size alone. Cottage gardens were small gardens (ideally a quarter acre) without any special style or 'look'. The back of the house was devoted to fruit and vegetable production and drying washing, while the front was for flowers, lawns, entrance paths and driveways which increasingly began to imitate middle- and upper-class designs which allowed for movement of vehicles and ostentatious display. Two typical designs can be seen in *Flower Gardening in New Zealand* by James Young and D. Hay (see fig. p. 30).[27] The design on the left shows the poorer classes aping the nobs by having a driveway which curves in a semi-circle in front of the house. In a grand garden, where the drive is flanked by large trees and flowering shrubs and the courtyard area in front of the house is large enough to hold three carriages with two horse teams in comfort, this looks gracious and appropriate. On a quarter acre it looks as out of scale as a top hat on a toddler. It might be redeemed if the semi-circular centre bed were lavishly planted with tall perennials or attractive shrubs, but in all the period photographs I have seen it never was.

If their designs were uninspired, Young and Hay nevertheless reiterated some principles of cottage gardening which are timeless. They include a sufficient rotation of plants to ensure beauty of bloom or foliage throughout the year; the maximum amount of colour and perfume obtained at minimum cost; a practical return for the labour and thought expended, and the growing of plants which combine utility with beauty in the flower garden as a background to hardy perennials: for example, trellises of green peas and runner beans, espaliers of berry fruits, and pyramid or bush fruit trees on the edge of a lawn.[28] Interestingly too, although Young and Hay state that 'The person with a quarter acre section should have as much grass as possible',[29] under 'Designing a Cottage Garden' they advise that 'unless the

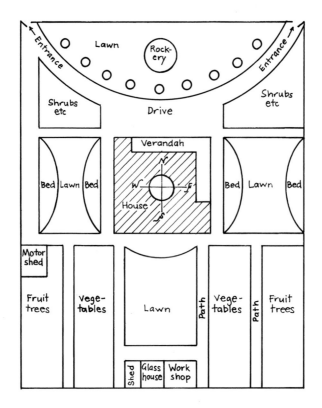
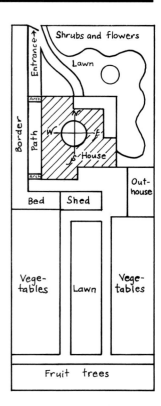

space permits, a lawn should not be attempted'. Perhaps they thought of cottage gardens as being smaller than a quarter acre.[30]

When it came to a style of growing flowers, Young and Hay were advocates of refining the horrid Victorian fashion of carpet bedding. Carpet bedding, as they describe it, is 'the regular and formal arrangement of dwarf foliage plants, hardy or tender, either by themselves or in combination with flowers. This term originated in the carpet-like flatness with which the arrangements were carried out at first.'[31] But now, say Young and Hay, 'this flatness is broken by the intermixing of tall foliage plants, and a better expression is used, viz. panel gardening.'[32] They then go on to advise that, in cold and wet districts, it would be too much to devote one half of the ground to this style of bedding, and they give extensive lists of suitable plants, suggested combinations and elaborate designs for beds. Beds never had more than five types of flowers, and the emphasis was on bright colours. Imagine the effect of a bed filled with Californian poppies, godetias in white and mixed colours, *Jacobea elegans* 'Alba' and blue lobelia, which is one of their cheery suggestions.

Herbaceous perennials and the herbaceous border receive less attention, and the advice given suggests that Young and Hay had not read William Robinson and Gertrude Jekyll. For example, they advise arranging the herbaceous border plants in lines 'graduated in height from front to back, and bold and telling plants should be planted at equal distances'. This is completely contrary to the successful Jekyll system, where plants are grouped in lozenge-shaped clumps parallel to the front of the border, heights are varied not graduated, and plants are not popped in like soldiers on sentry duty at equal intervals. Nor do Young and Hay advise on colour combinations for the herbaceous border, although this is really the point of this tricky type of

planting. It is, of course, harder to control the flowering and harmonising of perennials than annuals, and this may account for the popularity of summer bedding schemes, despite their predictability and garishness.

There were a few New Zealand gardeners ignoring or bucking the dominant early twentieth-century trend. We don't know how many working-class gardeners kept on with the old, mixed, cottage style, but we do know that there was a very prominent middle-class gardener who railed against the Victorian taste which had gripped England and then spread to New Zealand. This was the great botanist Leonard Cockayne, who grew up in Yorkshire in the 1860s, at a time when Victorian gardening was sweeping the landscape. This made such a negative impression on the young Cockayne that in a memoir written in his seventy-ninth year he recorded:

> To make way for this mockery of horticulture noble trees were cut to the ground, shrubberies were eradicated and the plants of which Shakespear [sic] wrote were rooted up and cast among the garden refuse. To the growing boy this style of gardening did not appeal; in fact he hated it; for he loved the few herbaceous borders and shrubberies near his home, those unmolested, and he admired the cottage gardens, often only a few square yards in extent, where many old favourites were well cared for.[33]

Thirty years later, when Cockayne began planting his 'unorthodox garden' on a four-and-a-half-acre property called Tarata at New Brighton, Christchurch, his love for perennials and dislike of annuals persisted: 'annuals usually were not to be admitted but notable exceptions were to be made in this regard.'[34] Cockayne reserved his affection for traditional 'come-again' flowers, his favourite of which was the daffodil. One hundred and forty-six varieties were blooming in his Wellington garden just before he died in 1934.

Cockayne, with his enthusiasm for native plants and cottage flowers, was way ahead of his time, and despite his active involvement in horticultural societies he does not seem to have had any influence on the dominant trend

in gardening between the two world wars. Far more influential were organisations like the Christchurch Beautifying Association, which instituted garden competitions in the 1930s and actively encouraged exposed front gardens with beds of bright annuals and lines of standard roses set on expanses of lawn. Cottage gardens, which need shelter for delicate flowers and tender fruits and vegetables, continued to flourish behind the tall hedges and fences which were anathema to the would-be 'beautifiers', but they were very unfashionable. One member of the Christchurch Beautifying Association went so far as to suggest that the people who kept them were a lower form of citizen.[35]

It is very fitting that someone descended from such a lower form of citizen should be writing to praise the cottage garden today. My paternal grandfather, Charles Dann, a nurseryman and gardener by trade, kept a cottage garden of mixed vegetables, fruit trees and flowers behind a high hedge right through the 1930s, and when that hedge was removed to widen the road he promptly planted another one. On the small lawn enhanced by the sheltered privacy of the second hedge the large Dann family exchanged gifts on Christmas day throughout the 1950s and 1960s. Small wonder that I have a good word to say for the cottage garden, even though the term was not known to me then.

Nor was it used by Elsie Morton in her 1944 book *Gardening's Such Fun!*, although the garden which she inherited from her mother in Green Lane, Auckland, was obviously a cottage garden. It was full of old-fashioned flowers growing riotously and a haven for birds, cats and Morton's niece. Morton herself had imbibed the true spirit of the cottage garden from her mother, and used her writing skill to express its essence:

The sun had not yet risen; it was only a little after five o'clock and the garden was still a place of mystery and soft shadows . . . The poppies rose in series of soft, rose-

'Lancashire Hero', c. 1850. This auricula is a tribute to the skill of the old florists and the quality of their flowers.

red waves from a pearly sea of dew that lay all over the garden. The tall foxgloves, mauve and pink and white, stood like sentries against the hedge, and the masses of eschscholzia, every golden blossom still tight furled, were unlit beacons in the grey and silver lake of dew . . . The sun rose higher, the pepper-tree became a tall and beauteous sylvan goddess, draped from crown to foot in golden lace . . . Row by row the poppies caught fire and became waves of scarlet leaping flame. You cannot get this wonderful effect with a single clump of poppies or one single row, which is the most that is usually permitted in a well-kept garden.

You must have beds and beds of poppies; you must love them so much that you are willing to let them take charge and run riot, blooming freely where they will. If you do this, you will be giving your garden over to children of the wild, for the poppy is a true adventurer and will go gypsying wherever the sweet will takes her. She will thrust up between the bricks; she will skip gaily into all your cherished borders with a twirl of her scarlet skirts; she is utterly lawless, laughter-loving and lovely. She will greet you with great flaring, wide-open crimson flowers like the blare of trumpets, with exquisitely frail white blooms edged and ruffled with softest pink. But to see your poppies at their best you must see them, not in the lawless loveliness of high noontide, but as I saw them that morning, soft and wistful, the silver dew of night still bowing their proud heads, the golden fingers of the sun stretched out to raise the faces of his children of the wild.

The rising sun shone not only on the poppies, but on larkspurs, rosy scarlet and blue, on golden marigolds and eschscholzias, on tall spires of foxgloves, all ringing their little bells together. There were sweet-williams too, of every shade, and deep purple pansies, stocks, geraniums, roses, white 'bride' lilies, pink fairy bells and cornflowers bluer than the bluest sky.[36]

Morton shared her gardening experiences with readers of the *New Zealand Herald*, and kept the cottage flag flying hopefully. Other gardening books and columns of the 1940s and 1950s, such as J. A. McPherson's *The Complete New Zealand Gardener*, tended to be practical compendiums containing all the down-to-earth information required by the suburban gardener. The more romantic side of gardening did not surface again until the 1960s, with the formation of herb clubs and societies. In this respect New Zealand was right up with the gardening play; most of the herb gardens in England which we think of as being traditional were actually planted after the Second World War as a result of the herb 'renaissance'.

Herb gardeners are first cousins to cottage gardeners, and the revival of interest in cottage gardening was probably sparked by the revival of interest in herbs. It was helped by the publication of books by women who were knowledgeable about the old-fashioned flowers and enthusiastic about natural, cottagey styles of gardening. They included Gilian Painter and Elaine Power (*The Herb Garden Displayed*, *A Garden of Old-fashioned and Unusual Herbs*), Nancy Steen (*The Charm of Old Roses*), Jean Lawrence (*A Garden Full of Wings*, *Gardening Tales*) and Kerry Carman (*Portrait of a Garden*). By the 1980s nurseries specialising in herbs, cottage plants and perennials were springing up like mushrooms, and cottage gardening in New Zealand had come 180 degrees round the circle, from essential to fashionable.

This book is a reflection of the revival of interest in cottage gardening, and enthusiasts may dream that one day we will go full circle, with cottage gardening once more an essential feature of the New Zealand way of life.

It's old – isn't it? New building and plant materials combined with old English elements to create this cottage garden in Napier in the 1880s. The gardener invites you to pick peas, figs and gooseberries among the Madonna lilies.

Chapter 4

Contemporary Cottage Gardening

The latter half of the twentieth century may well be remembered not as a glorious epoch (like the Age of Discovery, or the Age of Enlightenment) but as the age which was no age at all, because it was an era of instant-everything. Instant food, instant drink, instant communication, instant money, instant sex – and instant death. How relevant is the concept of the cottage garden to an era in which supermarkets and pharmacies instantly and cheaply dispense passable copies of the produce of a garden, while garden centres even supply the ornamental side of a garden (lawn, flowering plants, fully grown trees) on demand? Is the cottage garden an anachronism, soon doomed to go the way of the dodo? Or does it paradoxically have more relevance than ever, as the negative side of the Age of Instant becomes more and more apparent?

There is no doubt that for a small but enthusiastic minority of New Zealanders, cottage gardening is a vital aspect of their way of life, an important component of staying healthy and happy. I have met a number of elderly cottage gardeners but hesitate to call them retired, because they are so obviously fully engaged with life in their garden and outside it. Failing sight, arthritis, gammy legs and other problems of ageing are brushed aside as mere inconveniences rather than major deterrents to an active life. Seventy or eighty years young, these gardeners are still keen to keep up with the latest news, in gardening and in current events. They are just as interested in new varieties of plants and new, appropriate technologies as younger gardeners.

Young gardeners in contact with these inspiring older examples have no doubts about the models they are following, but perhaps feel more need to justify their practice of an 'old' style of gardening. The 'Small is Beautiful' rationale of the 1960s and 1970s was totally out of fashion by the 1980s, leaving cottage gardeners under forty way out of step with the yuppie ethos of their peers. Small gardens with exotic and/or expensive features (topiary, daisies in terracotta pots, spa pools, potted palms, sculpture, and so on) were in, but self-sufficiency-style gardens were out. Old-fashioned English perennials were making a comeback, but chiefly in imitative English-style borders,

*The stunning Chatham Island forget-me-not (*Myosotidium hortensia*).*
OLAF JOHN

rather than as components of an overall cottage design. Paradoxically, the cottage gardeners were making more use of New Zealand native plants than the trendies.

Cottage gardeners were as usual unfazed by whether they were in fashion or not, finding that fresh flavoursome food, choice flowers, gentle remedies, natural perfumes, healthy recreation and peaceful surroundings are their own reward. Cottage gardens have been meeting all these requirements for centuries, and still no better substitute has been found. Certainly not an instant one. As long as people who appreciate these things are with us, the cottage garden will be with us, a lively tradition still relevant to today.

Alistair Isdale, New Zealand's first commercial herb nurseryman, expressed it this way: 'To be really progressive requires a great knowledge of history, the best way of improving on the present usually being found in the multitudinous past, the direct capacity of the imagination being limited.'[1] But just who is the contemporary cottage gardener, what sort of garden does she or he have, and what is grown in a New Zealand cottage garden?

The Contemporary Cottage Gardener

The rural labouring couple of yesteryear, using their small amounts of free time and land to be self-sufficient in fruit, vegetables and herbs, and perhaps poultry and honey, would seem to have little in common with cottage gardeners in New Zealand today. Most of us live in towns and cities, work in the secondary or tertiary sectors of the economy, have at least two days of leisure time per week and can buy everything a garden can produce at reasonable prices.

On the other hand, we are renowned for our 'do-it-yourself' tradition, developed at a time when imported alternatives were not available. The urge to do things for ourselves is common to all cottage gardeners, past and present. Even when it is not essential to survival, it is satisfying. However, it seems that this impulse is now stronger in women than in men, for about two-thirds of the cottage gardeners who referred themselves or were referred to me were female. Growers of cottage garden plants also report that at least two-thirds of their customers are female.

Is this because women as a whole garden more than men, or because cottage gardening as a style appeals to us particularly? Certainly many of the products of the traditional cottage garden (preserves, pot-pourri, herbal remedies, and so on) require skills which have, up till now, been encouraged in women but not in men. There also seems to be a connection between an interest in herbs (which in New Zealand is largely a female interest) and an interest in the full range of traditional cottage garden plants.

One female cottage gardener thought that cottage gardening suited women because they prefer 'bitsier' gardens; men, she said, have 'tidier minds'! Another said bluntly, 'Men like lawns and drains.' Growers report that husbands are frequently impatient of their wives dallying in the nursery, and like shrubs rather than flowers in their gardens. One mail-order nursery finds that male customers are more likely to be plant connoisseurs who make collections of one type, whereas female customers seem to like a bit of everything.

The centrepiece of the cottage garden at Sissinghurst, showing the strong design features of a well-planned garden.

This information is not intended to discourage men from cottage gardening. There is nothing to prevent men from acquiring the processing skills which would enable them to derive maximum productive benefit from their cottage garden, and among the male cottage gardeners I visited I noticed a willingness to experiment which bodes well for the future of cottage gardening in New Zealand. These days both sexes are breaking the hidebound tradition of vege gardening for men and flower gardening for women. Women are now eagerly growing new and unusual varieties of vegetables and men are encouraging flowers everywhere, even in the vege patch.

Apart from the (shifting) gender difference, there is no easy way to spot a New Zealand cottage gardener. You have to see their gardens, and start asking questions about their gardening philosophy, to discover if they are true cottage gardeners or not.

The ancient art of topiary was kept alive by cottagers. Many fine examples still exist and the art is enjoying a current resurgence of interest.

Contemporary Cottage Garden Principles

The cottage garden in New Zealand today is defined mainly by function, not by facade. Some cottage gardeners have artistic training or inclinations and their gardens are truly pictures, viewed from any angle and in any season. Light and shade, flowers and foliage, tones of colour are all skilfully placed to create the moods the gardener is seeking. Even vege gardens can be designed to look good, and fruit trees can contribute to beauty as well as production in a well-designed garden. Other cottage gardeners, however, love their plants as individuals, and plant them without much thought of the overall visual effect. They would seem to have little in common with the design-conscious gardeners, but after interviewing nearly fifty cottage gardeners, I found that regardless of whether their garden emphasised the artistic, the productive or the botanical, they shared several common features. These are the best guidelines I can offer to those wanting to identify or create an authentic New Zealand cottage garden. All are based on the unifying principle of cottage gardening: the combination of utility and beauty.

1. The cottage garden is productive

Cottage gardeners definitely garden for produce. However, by produce they don't necessarily mean just apples, spuds and cabbages. They also mean fruits from plants usually grown for ornament, such as japonica 'apples', elderberries, rosehips, sunflower seeds and chamomile flowers. Vegetables might include neglected and unusual varieties, and plants which most people think of as weeds (puwha, dandelion, chickweed) or flowers (nasturtium, chrysanthemum, borage). Artichokes appear in the flower borders because their leaves are ornamental; marigolds find space in the vege patch because their petals are edible. Bay trees can go anywhere and be both useful and decorative. Herbs and flowers also lead a double life, masquerading as ornamentals one moment and being shorn for processing in the kitchen the next. The productive garden is not necessarily or only row upon row of regimented veges and fruit trees: cottage gardening is the art of producing more things and different things, in a more relaxed way. The distinction between 'ornamental' and 'productive' is blurred.

Natural materials give much better results than artificial alternatives. Here stone steps are softened with clumps of primulas and rock plants.

2. The cottage garden is practical

Cottage gardeners eschew unnecessary frills and fripperies. They have no time for statues, fountains, wishing wells and other artificial forms of garden ornamentation. They might succumb to an occasional small ornament – but usually as a joke. A cottage garden is for plants, not plaster of Paris. Cottage gardens are laid out to suit the *convenience* of the busy gardener, so neat paths, well-edged beds, sturdy compost bins and so on are never out of fashion. However, they need not render a garden hopelessly dull and prosaic. Sometimes the convenience of the gardener (her desire for privacy perhaps, or his wish to grow naturalised bulbs) dictates winding paths and wild corners, and these are equally 'cottagey'. More often, any element of formality or stodginess introduced by the utilitarian ground plan of a cottage garden is rapidly obscured when Principle 3 comes into play.

3. A cottage garden is profuse

A cottage gardener loves plants. If the old adage, 'The more the merrier' is true, then the cottage garden is one of the most cheerful places on earth. You

39

An early sod dwelling and a wonderfully profuse cottage garden in the Waimata Valley, 1890.
GISBORNE MUSEUM COLLECTION

may assume that all gardeners like plants – why else would they garden? – but if you compare the average New Zealand suburban garden with a true cottage garden you will find a big difference in the number of species and varieties grown. Wealthy cottage gardeners are always poring over catalogues and collecting new treasures from mail-order nurseries; hard-up cottage gardeners are whizzes at propagating plants from seed and cuttings bludged from friends and acquaintances. A cottage gardener knows much more about propagation than most suburban gardeners, who buy the bulk of their limited range of plants ready grown from a garden centre.

Nor does the cottage garden confine its greater range of plant material to conventional beds and borders. Even when grown in beds and borders, cottage garden plants are permitted, often encouraged, to spill over on to paths and lawns. They are also allowed everywhere else in the garden. In the lawn, daisies, speedwell, lotus and other creeping gems are tolerated. Indeed, instead of conventional lawn, thyme, chamomile, pratia, jewel mint or heather are charming alternatives, greener, prettier or less work than grass. Naturalised in long grass and under trees, bulbs and corms can grow in any season, from late-winter snowflakes through to late-autumn cyclamens. Growing over the house, sheds, garages and other utilitarian structures, old-fashioned climbers like roses, honeysuckle, clematis and jasmine grow freely, and newer treasures like hardenbergia and kohia give a year-round coverage of flowers and foliage. There's a place, too, for the 'double-duty' vines and climbers like grape, kiwifruit and passionfruit. Old trees are not cut down, but are pressed into service to support climbers; old containers like sinks and babies' baths are never thrown away but are filled with earth and then plants.

We all know, perhaps by some atavistic instinct, that the Garden of Eden was more like a jungle than a lawn bounded by neatly clipped shrubs and regimented begonias in bare beds. There is little in the typical suburban style of garden to tempt Adam, Eve or any number of serpents. A profusely planted garden, to those of us brought up with visions of Eden, may always seem more beautiful, and this may account for the evergreen attraction of the cottage garden.

4. The cottage garden is ecologically sensitive

In order to be productive, the cottage garden must be fertile and healthy. For over 500 years cottage gardeners have maintained soil fertility by using organic manures and fertilisers – animal wastes and composted plant material. This method of maintaining soil fertility is cheap, easy and totally sustainable. Then along came inorganic fertilisers – expensive, difficult (for people like me who find measuring and computing weights by area tedious and tricky) and unsustainable. Unsustainable because inorganic fertilisers are derived from non-renewable resources such as oil and rock and because they return nothing to the soils to which they are applied, and thus are part of the process of topsoil loss, which is now an international environmental problem.

So why are they so widely used? It certainly takes less effort to sprinkle a powder than to apply organic manures. There is also no doubt that correctly applied doses of the right inorganic chemical mix can boost crop yields – at least until the soil structure collapses because it has not received enough organic matter to build it up.

Cottage gardeners enjoy the labour involved in making or transporting organic manures and fertilisers (it's a lot more rewarding than jazzercise) and think it is criminal to destroy the soil of tomorrow for the sake of an extra handful of beans today. Gardens using inorganic chemicals for maximum production are like athletes taking steroids to win gold medals – there is a price to be paid some day. A good cottage gardener is a good organic gardener, and Chapter 7 of this book gives advice on how to become both.

Gardening organically means gardening without synthetic poisons as well as without synthetic fertilisers. Weeds, pests and diseases can all be controlled without toxic chemicals that can have drastic short-term effects on humans as well as on both pest and beneficial species, and unknown long-term effects. The home gardener can easily sustain any slight losses in yields or imperfections in produce which are currently unacceptable to the commercial grower. Spraying with toxic chemicals is for ignorant gardeners, the ones who don't know enough about the flora and fauna in their garden to keep the good ones in optimum health and the bad ones on the run through proper management techniques. Cottage gardeners start smart and end up wise. Their gardens not only look good and smell good, they are good for you.

This is the garden at Mount Vernon, in the United States, which George Washington knew in the late eighteenth century. Here classic cottage plants are framed by ancient clipped box hedges and edging.

MOUNT VERNON LADIES
ASSOCIATION

Chapter 5

Designing Your Cottage Garden

Dianthus nitidus

The traditional English cottage garden grew organically in more ways than one. As time, money and the cultivation of gift plants allowed, plantings were increased and extended. With many of the plants originally wild, and the style of planting informal, the cottage garden often seemed merely a more floriferous version of the surrounding countryside, with only the most simple elements of conscious design. By the nineteenth century, however, even cottage gardens were deliberately designed to be more useful and more beautiful, and it makes sense to study these principles of design before embarking on creating a cottage garden. It will save time, effort and money, and should result in a more attractive and productive garden.

Good garden design starts with a consideration of key questions which are universal. Whether you are creating a garden for a cottage or a castle, you must ask and answer practical, aesthetic and horticultural questions. These are asked below, and where specifically 'cottage garden' answers are appropriate, these are given.

Practical Questions

Who are you making a cottage garden for? The cottage garden answer is 'yourself and your household'. Your satisfaction is paramount. If you wish to present a cottagey display to passersby we will all love you for it, but a cottage gardener should not feel compelled to be a public gardener as well. You should lay out your garden to provide maximum use and beauty for yourself.

The next question may sound pretentious, but for anyone who sees gardening as the most common and popular interface between art and science, it is not so silly. It is: 'Who am I?' Are you a busy person who wants a low-maintenance garden? A conservationist who wants to grow rare and old-fashioned plants? An artist who wants to paint with plants? An ecologist fascinated by habitats? A rose lover? An owner of cats or dogs, or a bird-watcher? A retired person who wants to spend hours in the garden? Most occupations and lifestyles are quite compatible with cottage gardening, but before you start on a style of gardening which may ultimately frustrate you,

All the cottage flowers you could want – love-lies-bleeding, nicotiana, pansies, violas and sunflowers thriving in their new home.
HOCKEN LIBRARY

it is worth comparing your own attributes with the attributes of a typical cottage gardener and seeing if there is a match or a mismatch.

A cottage garden is a 'self-reliance' garden. It consists of plants which can flourish with a minimum of assistance or interference, and then reward the gardener with flowers and fruit. This suits the typically self-reliant cottage gardener, who gets a thrill out of making his own preserves or propagating her own plants.

It is a natural garden – a haven for birds, bees and butterflies, maintained by ecologically sound means with a minimum of machinery and chemicals.

It is a relaxed garden, where plants sprawl over paths, drape themselves over trees and buildings, bubble out of the cracks in walls and paving, and look sad and miserable if told to stand up straight and pull themselves together.

It is a garden for gardeners who think of gardening as recreation, not labour.

So, if your real interest is choice plants which require special attention, and you'd rather buy your food at the supermarket and your plants at the garden centre, build a rock garden or a glasshouse and forget the cottage garden idea. If bees make you nervous, birds irritate you, and butterflies make you reach for the spraycan, stick to conifers or grass. If your fingers itch to cut back 'untidy' plants and make everything neat and straight, cottage gardening is not for you. If you currently delight in scalping hedges with a chainsaw and spraying at the first sign of a weed or pest, can you make the transition to turning compost and companion planting for your practical garden pleasures?

You might be happy with a cottage garden. But what about your household? The next step in planning a cottage garden is to ask what compromises you need to make with the other functions your garden may be required to perform. These include providing play space for children, parking and turning for cars, enclosures for animals, and so on. Perhaps you want to entertain in your garden: if so, do you want to give barbecues or tea parties? Do you need shelter and privacy for sunbathing? These requirements will vary from household to household, and you will have to design your garden around them. If you add them as afterthoughts they have a tendency to stick out like sore thumbs. If you deal with them first, you can find ways of integrating them into the overall scheme.

Then come the practical requirements of the garden itself – compost bins, tool shed, glasshouse, water taps. What do you need, what can you afford and what are the best sites for these basic facilities?

Next, an appraisal of what you want most from your garden. Is your priority flowers, fruit or vegetables? In what proportions? You should allocate your ground accordingly, choosing the best aspects for your priority crops.

What about labour? A cottage gardener is usually an amateur with only evenings and weekends to spare. If you are the only gardener, how much time do you have and what can you realistically cope with? Do you want to spend every spare minute in your garden, or do you need to think of ways (such as leaving or designing part of your garden as 'wilderness') which will save labour? Do you have any special needs and how can they be met? If, for example, you are disabled or merely disinclined to stoop a lot, raised beds will make gardening easier for you.

Designing a garden is no different from designing a home. Unless the life-style of the occupants is taken into consideration, and the invisible essentials such as plumbing and wiring are properly accounted for, the house is at best inconvenient and at worst downright uncomfortable. So start by consulting your convenience and building your garden from the bottom up.

Aesthetic Questions

Cottage gardens attract some people because they seem more 'beautiful' than other styles of gardening. What does this beauty consist of? Why should drifts of flowers, clumps of herbs and gnarled fruit trees be considered more beautiful than a perfectly kept lawn or a planting of conifers? That yearning for the primeval garden again . . . ?

Preferring natural profusion is one thing – achieving that effect in an urban or suburban garden is another. If you scatter some packets of 'cottage garden' seed over bare ground you will *not* end up with a cottage garden. You will end up with an interesting experiment into which species are most hardy in your soil and climate conditions – and it will probably look like a dog's breakfast. So, what aesthetic questions do you need to ask to get a beautiful as well as a useful garden?

Sense of place

As I've already said and intend to say again, to be truly beautiful a garden should complement the landscape, not contradict it. The father of English flower gardening, William Robinson, put it this way in his best-seller, *The English Flower Garden*:

What is the use of Essex going into Dorset merely to see the same thing done in the home landscape or the garden? But if Essex were to study his own ground and do the best he could from his own knowledge of the spot, his neighbour might be glad to see his garden. We have too much of the stereotyped style already; in nine cases out of ten we can tell beforehand what we are going to see in a country place in the way of conventional garden design and planting; and clearly that is not art in any right sense of the word and never can be.[1]

New Zealanders can learn a lesson from Robinson, for New Zealand has more climatic variation than England and a greater range of landscape types. But when almost everything will grow well here, it is very hard to sort out what suits us best, and most suburban gardeners have shirked the task and opted for a limited range of stiff and bright plants arranged formally around the ubiquitous lawn.

The cottage gardener can do better than this, and must begin by consulting the *genius loci*, or spirit of the place. This is not difficult for anyone in possession of the six senses: sight, hearing, touch, taste, smell – and imagination. What was on the land before your street was surveyed or your section subdivided? What is there now? Is what is there now in harmony with what

Profusion in a country setting – the quintessential cottage garden.

would have been there if it had been left to nature? Can you recapture or reinforce that sense of naturalness, of rightness, of fitting in?

Does water – sea, stream or lake – contribute to the *genius loci*, or is it wind, sun, mountain or forest?

It is obviously foolish to plant marram grass in the mountains or eidelweiss on the seashore, but what more subtle messages is your site giving you about what is appropriate to it? For example, why do rhododendrons, plants from the Asian mountains, look natural in South Otago and unnatural in Hawke's Bay? How come Californian and Mediterranean pines look good on Banks Peninsula but off-key in Westland? Why do eucalypts look at home in Marlborough, but lacklustre in Northland? Probably it is because such plants *could* have evolved in these environs, and they don't have to make a major adjustment to their new home. There is a real and subtle art in working with and not against your climate and landforms, and it is well worth the effort to research plants from other countries which can adapt gracefully to your local site. If the subject really interests you, read Russell Page's *The Education of a Gardener* for some very wise words on why and how establishing a firm sense of place matters in the creation of a good garden.

Simplicity

Another aesthetic factor which Page stresses as being inextricably linked with the realisation of the *genius loci* is simplicity. Bright and ornate objects are not necessarily gross and ugly, as we know from seeing folk embroideries, for example, but they are never peaceful, restful or harmonious in the way that objects with simpler lines and softer colours are. Gardens can of course be designed to startle, shock, enliven, amuse – and if you like that kind of garden you will adore the famous Tiger Balm Gardens in Singapore, where coloured concrete largely replaces plants. The cottage garden is obviously not such a garden, and while in summer it may be bright and cheerful with flower colour, at all times of the year it should emphasise balance rather than busyness. It is a garden for *being in*, whether for digging, weeding, harvesting, pruning, strolling, reading, chatting or resting, rather than a garden for viewing and visiting.

Do you really want to live in the horticultural equivalent of a jewellery boutique or confectionery shop – a floor-to-ceiling experience of bright, fussy, contrived colour and form, all crammed into a small space? In your initial enthusiasm for the great range of cottage garden plants, such excess is a definite temptation – and one which can be guarded against only by careful attention to the purpose of your garden. If you keep it simple, you will be more successful, especially in a small area where there is room only for one, perhaps two, dominant themes. Roy Strong offers excellent advice in his inspiring book, *Creating Small Gardens*: 'The relationship of small garden design to interior decoration is an extremely valid one. No room can contain more than one coordinated theme. The smaller a garden is, the closer to a room it becomes and the lesson on a unifying theme . . . is reinforced.'[2]

How do you follow this advice? By a process of elimination. List all the features you want most in your garden – and then list them again and again, in order of priority, until your heart's deepest desire is revealed. Of course you want roses and lilies and an orchard and a fish pond and a bird bath and a dovecote and a herb garden and a shrubbery and . . . But if you try to fit them all on a quarter acre, all you'll have will be a cramped collection and not a real garden. So what do you want most? A bower of roses? Apples 'in hatfuls and in capfuls and in bushel bags and all, and the cider running out of every gutter hole'? Water reflecting, running or rippling? A green apothecary's shop? An aviary without wires, full of song and fluttering?

Some of these choices will mesh (birds in orchards, water in a rose garden) and others will be incompatible (English herbs and New Zealand birds, lots of water and lots of trees). Your job is to choose the optimum combination for you. Your guiding principle should be to select the one thing or two things which you can do really well – and then go to town. If it's apples, grow twenty different varieties, not just in an orchard but all over the garden. If it's roses, arrange to have them flowering from September through to June, in beds, in borders, in shrubberies, up trees and pergolas, over the shed, the garage and the house. If it's herbs, design a special garden for them.

Although the cottage garden is a multi-purpose garden, intended for production as well as relaxation, there is no reason why it should be *bitsy*. A flourishing thicket of trees and shrubs native to the area will be more authentically 'cottage' (as well as more authentically New Zealand) than a few bitsy beds in a drought-stricken lawn containing one or two struggling representatives of twenty or thirty traditional English cottage plant genera.

Keeping it simple is extremely difficult in the Age of Instant when so much that is cheap, easy and nasty is thrust upon our consciousness, claiming to be the latest which we can't do without. If you already practise a technique for slowing down and tuning into the eternal, creative principle (regardless of what you call it and whether your technique is prayer, meditation, yoga, Tai Chi or something else), you will find the gentle contemplation of what is truly beautiful and useful in a garden is complementary

This driftwood archway and fencing are fine examples of New Zealand cottage ingenuity.
WILKINSON COLLECTION, ALEXANDER TURNBULL LIBRARY

to it. If you don't have such a technique, maybe thinking about your garden will be a starting point or a substitute.

Colour

Colour is not inherent in objects but is a function of light. Anyone who has spent a whole day in a garden will know that flower and foliage colours look different under morning, noonday and evening light. This fact holds true for both northern and southern hemispheres, and sophisticated gardeners take it into account when deciding where to place certain plants.

It is well worth thinking about the ways in which you can use light to enhance colour in your garden. Virginia creepers, for example, are traditionally grown against a wall, but if they (or any of the other vines with brilliant autumn foliage) are grown over a pergola or in a tree through which the afternoon sun shines, they will provide an even more glorious display.

Dappled light is often more effective than direct light in suggesting the delicacy of a planting of small bulbs, and really experienced gardeners in warm gardens where evening strolls and sitting out late are feasible will also give thought to the different quality of moonlight. Pale blues can appear white, and whites become luminescent.

Several garden writers have covered the subject of the nature of colour and light and its relevance to good gardening in depth – I can recommend Gertrude Jekyll, Stephen Lacey, Kerry Carman and Penelope Hobhouse (see Bibliography). It is a fascinating area of study for those who have got the horticultural basics under control and now want to turn a good garden into an inspired one. It should, however, always be remembered that light in New Zealand is very different from light in Europe. Any well-read and observant person who has visited Britain will have been delighted to see the colour adjectives used by British writers suddenly making sense – *iron* grey sea, for example, I had always dismissed as artist's hyperbole until I saw the English Channel in winter. Similarly, European film-makers in the Antipodes find the strength and clarity of southern light a shock after the diffuse, gentle haziness of northern skies. This difference in the quality of light between north and south means that New Zealand gardeners cannot take the guidelines on colour laid down by British gardeners as gospel. So what new rules of thumb are appropriate for New Zealand conditions?

Gertrude Jekyll, pioneer and prophet of co-ordinated colour schemes in garden borders, has been the model most consulted by gardeners striving for the glorious effects she achieved. New Zealanders who have attempted to follow her schemes, however, have come to the conclusion that they are wrong for us. In her long borders, Jekyll aimed for a gentle colour display in spring, gradually rising to a flame of glory in mid to late summer. Liz Brunsden, a cottage gardener in Te Puke, has tried and rejected this system in her garden. Other gardeners in northern New Zealand echo her distaste for a welter of bright colours in summer. They are understandable in England, where they may serve to warm and brighten dull summer days; in New Zealand they are impossibly hot and harsh. So in summer Liz sticks to the cooler colours (mainly blues and whites) for the bulk of her planting, and uses tiny pockets of bright colours (yellow, crimson and magenta, but not

ABOVE:

The essence of good garden design is the creation of a series of garden pictures. Here at Sissinghurst the massed apricot foxgloves blend beautifully with the background cottage – making an unforgettable picture.

RIGHT:

This combination of salmon-pink roses and old Elizabethan bricks illustrates the potential of harmonising flower colour with building elements.

Theme planting can produce stunning effects. White and silver is a popular choice, with the White Garden at Sissinghurst, pictured here, a trendsetter for this style of gardening.

orange or scarlet) to lift her planting schemes. Paradoxically, however, it does not pay to go too pale. In *The Creative Gardener* Kerry Carman warns against taking Gertrude Jekyll's pastel planting schemes literally. They can appear too washed-out in our intense light, and need supplementing with deeper tones to give depth to a planting.

Colour-conscious New Zealand cottage gardeners are showing a preference for restricting bulk plantings of the bright colours to spring and late autumn when their warmth is welcome, gladdening the eye rather than searing it. The North Island enthusiasm for all-white gardens apparent at the time of researching this book, although undoubtedly a tediously derivative steal from the famous white garden at Sissinghurst, may not be just another useless imported concept. While a completely white garden is quite unnatural, and hence uncottagey, and anyone who copies the Sissinghurst garden idea complete with weeping silver pears and white statues deserves a perpetual plague of greenfly for not thinking for themselves, a garden which reverses the English dictum of using white to bring up the colours and instead uses colour to bring up the white may be worth considering. Especially fitting in a country where most of the native flowers are white, such a style offers a way of combining refined sensibilities with earthy common sense.

In foliage as well as flower colour, New Zealand natives are ideally suited for cooling down gardens. You cannot pick up an English garden book these days without seeing *Senecio greyii* mentioned as the ideal, all-purpose, silver-leafed shrub, yet here it is mainly used to shore up unpromising banks and rarely given a chance to show its worth in a properly conceived planting scheme. As for hebes – it is extremely frustrating to read in Robin Lane Fox's *Better Gardening* of ideal garden varieties which are not available here, the home of hebes.

In a climate where hot colour is easily achieved, it seems we need to think more about the value of cool colour. The study of an interaction of colour and light in New Zealand gardening is very much in its infancy, and it may be that the ideas I have put forward will be rejected by present or future generations of gardeners who glory in startling displays of colour at the hottest times of the year. Anyone who is familiar with Christchurch front gardens blazing wth dahlias, African marigolds and geraniums in February will know that the handling of colour I have suggested is quite contrary to the current gardening ethos in the Garden City.

Since cottage gardeners are neither trendsetters nor followers they need not worry about their lack of conformity. Perhaps the only invariable guide-line for choice of colour in the cottage garden is the awareness that the cottage garden is for *living* in. If your living-room walls are red and your furniture orange you can probably handle a hot, bright garden. Most of us opt for more subtle shades inside and out. The traditional cottage garden flowers come in pure, refined colours, and can easily be blended with native New Zealand foliage to produce a restful and harmonious whole, with pockets of stimulating colour placed and timed to appear just where and when you need them.

Timing

Timing is of course crucial both to the management of colour in the garden and to the sense of unity and progression which a garden should convey throughout the year. In most parts of New Zealand there are four distinct seasons, and our gardens should celebrate the seasonal changes.

Daffodils should appear as a healthy horde in September, not as a drooping dozen in December. Christmas lilies and cherries should arrive by Christmas Day, not Twelfth Night. Winter sweet and winter roses should appear as refined treats in the July garden.

Under normal weather conditions it should not be too difficult to replicate this reassuring sense of Nature going about her business in a natural way. Most garden manuals will tell you when to plant a particular species, and how long it takes for it to flower or fruit. Getting the month right is not usually a problem, but those who are gardening for combined colour effects often want to get the week right. It is obviously not possible to give nation-wide rules for such exact timing – to say, for instance, that your blue delphiniums will be tall and floriferous enough by the last week of November to provide a good backing for your pink and white paeonies. In Otago, with warmth and rain, they might be. In Wellington, with cool, dry weather, they might not. Or vice versa.

The easiest way out of this problem (and one which Gertrude Jekyll did not despise) is to opt for plants with long flowering periods so that you can

Colonial symmetry – corrugated iron enhanced by clove pinks running in borders for the full length of the gravel path. This photograph was taken on the East Cape in the early 1900s.

GISBORNE MUSEUM COLLECTION

be guaranteed an overlap. This means that you must research your plantings not only for colour, form and size, but also for length of flowering. *Salvia uliginosa* and *Gaura lindheimeri*, for instance, will go on and on saying 'blue and white' at you until you're tempted to tell them to shut up, but you might prefer this to fiddling with a choice early delphinium and a late white tulip which say their piece so fast you barely have time to catch it before it is gone.

Creating effects with short-lived flowers is for gardeners who like exercising (or showing off) their skills. Beautiful and authentic cottage gardens are created by gardeners who get plants to work for them, rather than getting themselves to work for the plants. This does not mean that you must banish all evanescent gems. Just site them where their effect is not dependent on co-operation with other tricky flowers.

Horticultural Questions

You have designed your garden to make appropriate allocations for utilities, fruit, vegetables, herbs and flowers. You have established your fruit and vegetable priorities and made provision for their cultural needs. You approach the ornamental side of your garden somewhat more anxiously, knowing that there are hundreds of plants to choose from, with a great range of cultural requirements. How do you choose what is best for you? You do it by a process of elimination, which proceeds in the following manner:

Aspect

Is the area you want to plant sunny or shady, hot or cold, wet or dry? Make an accurate assessment of what types of plants will be happy there, and then 'go with the flow'. Don't put sun-loving plants in the shade and moisture-loving plants on hot, dry banks. I know this sounds a bit elementary, but I am still surprised at how many good (and expensive) plants come to a sad and shrivelled end because the person planting them did not consult their requirements at the outset. I confess that in my eagerness to get things in the ground I have done this myself, and only got round to consulting the manual when the plant began to tell me by its drooping leaves that it wasn't happy where I had put it. So now I look it up first, and check out its soil and fertiliser requirements at the same time.

What say it isn't in your manual? As you get to know what questions to ask your plants, you will be able to read their answers. Plants adapted to hot, sunny sites have had to adopt strategies to conserve water. These include small leaves, hard stalks, 'furry' or tough leaves, silvery or greyish foliage. Plants adapted to damp, shady places give opposite signals – large, fleshy leaves, juicy stalks, deep green colouring. Look at your new plant carefully, compare it with similar plants in your garden, and if you want to enhance your reputation for delightful eccentricity ask it, 'Where would you like to live?' It is not potty to talk to plants if by so doing you learn to listen to what they are silently saying. Of course, you can also ask your plant supplier – and check at the same time that the plant has been raised in optimum conditions.

If your garden is all sunny, or all shady, you may be tempted to sneak in a few misfits just because you love them so. This can be done, but not in the main plantings. With the bulk of the planting it is better to try to rein-

force the sunny or shady theme of your garden by selecting choice plants which will flourish only in your particular conditions. Visitors should be so busy envying your hostas or kingcups that it won't occur to them to lament the lack of rock roses. The place for contradictions to your theme is close to the house, in containers, in a specially created environment. Otherwise, it is best to let aspect be your first design adviser.

Soil

Your soil can be your next adviser. Is it mainly sand or mainly clay? Acid, alkaline or neutral? With the application of lots of compost and other forms of humus you can build up sand and break down clay, but do you need to go to all that effort? It is amazing how many plants will grow in pure sand, as New Zealand's luxuriant seaside gardens testify. Clay is more difficult, and more effort is required, so look for plants that won't shirk their duty. And don't shirk your duty to lighten the soil.

Acid soils can be made neutral or alkaline with applications of lime, and alkaline soil can be made neutral or acid with the addition of peat and leaf mould, but again you should ask yourself if it is worth the effort to make the change. For vegetables such applications are necessary in order to get good crops, because vegetables dislike acid and alkaline extremes. But for ornamentals it makes as little design sense as trying to fight the aspect. What does well naturally should be allowed to do its best. Confine any misfits you can't bear to forgo to small formal beds or containers near the house, where they can receive the special attention they require.

Cultural requirements

If you have chosen your plants according to their preferences for aspect and soil, their additional cultural requirements (fertiliser, water) will not be too difficult to satisfy. Cottage garden plants can be found for every type of situation, so cultural requirements should not be a very strict adviser.

Environment

As suggested in Chapter 4, be sensitive to your surroundings. Aim to blend in rather than show off. When looking at trees and shrubs, the big elements in your garden which form a framework for the smaller plants, let local plantings guide your choice (although only insofar as local plantings themselves enhance rather than contradict the wider environment). With such a wide and lovely range to choose from, it is hard to remember that one well-chosen, well-proportioned tree will set the tone of a cottage garden far more effectively than a hotch-potch planting. It is awfully difficult to get rid of trees which spoil a design theme once you have got used to them (and you'll most likely have to endure cries of 'Call yourself a conservationist!' or 'You'll touch that tree over my dead body!' if you suggest cutting anything down). So before you plant a tree, do consult some other gardens and tree books to make sure you choose the right one, and know where to plant it so that its removal becomes unthinkable.

History

Your neighbourhood will have its own history of gardening, and while you will not care for all the trends which have come and gone, another valid source of advice is what you see around you. Investigate local varieties of plants and keep them going. If your suburb is noted for pohutukawas, plant another one. It will reinforce the theme, and be there to carry on when an old one finally crumbles away. If you are going to grow roses, why not concentrate on the old species? As mass-market preferences for apples with tough, shiny skins, hard flesh and dubious taste reduce the range available to the consumer, grow the sweet and tender alternatives in your home orchard.

The cottage gardener of old was sometimes too conservative, sticking to a limited repertoire of plants merely from reluctance to make the effort to evaluate change. The cottage gardener of today, faced with incessant and rapid change, must make the effort, and may legitimately use historical associations and traditional uses as yet another guide to setting limits on the plants she or he should grow.

Aesthetic effect

This source of guidance has been left till last because it is the most variable. No plant is inherently ugly, yet preferences for individual plants, and combinations of plants, vary widely. Once you have decided on the sorts of aesthetic effects you want to achieve – cloudy drifts of white to lighten a bright bank, a blue haze highlighted with yellow and white to cool down a hot corner, a blur of colours to be seen from a ground-floor window, a formal pattern to be seen from an upstairs window, a busy botanical collection, a sense of still green restfulness, the mystery of a jungle – you must start to research the plants which will give you these effects.

For a cottage garden you will choose from the tried and true range of cottage plants listed and illustrated in this book, perhaps with the addition of New Zealand native plants (pp. 71–86) which suit cottage-style plantings. All sorts of combinations are possible, and it is recommended that with the aid of this and other books with pictures and descriptions of flowering plants you practise the type of planning exercises described later in this chapter.

No space is left unused in this Napier garden of the 1880s.

You should also study carefully how Nature achieves her own aesthetic effects and follow her rules of thumb. These include:

• Planting in groups. Plants in nature form colonies as seedlings spread out from the parent plant. If you imitate this habit your plantings will look more natural, so plant in drifts or clumps, not rows and squares. If you can manage only a few plants, make sure they are an odd number. Odd numbers look less neat and symmetrical and therefore less artificial than even numbers.

• Mixing colours. You may be tempted to get refined aesthetic effects by restricting plantings to one or two colours. This is all very well in great gardens with many 'rooms', but it tends to look at best dull and at worst forced in a cottage garden. Neither will it necessarily achieve the effect you desire. If you want to make a blue statement, the best way to emphasise the blue is to include a little yellow or orange in the planting. The contrast will highlight the dominant colour. Red tulips look even redder rising out of a mist of blue *Centaurea montana*, say, and pink roses are thrown into relief by the mauve and silver of lavender and *Stachys lanata* edgings.

However, having said that Nature mixes colours, it must also be said that Nature does not have access to the very bright modern hybrids, nor the opportunity to put a bright red lily from South Africa next to a big yellow daisy from North America. Your cottage garden of mixed colours will look neither natural nor restful if the strongest colours are jumbled up together. Lots of green foliage is needed to provide a foil for bright colours. If you love strong colours and live in a warm part of New Zealand you could forget about striving for delicate pastel blurs and go for a lush tropical effect with plants which look more natural in hot climates, such as bougainvillea, strelitzia, hibiscus, canna lilies, and so on, set off with lots of palms, ferns and other dramatic foliage plants.

One good way to mix colours is to let Nature do it for you. In this case Nature disdains perfectionists and favours the beginner. I thought I could tell different kinds of bulbs apart, so how did those two beautiful red tulips and a little clump of bluebells get into the bed where I planted (I thought) only daffodils? I don't mind – they look great contrasted with the blue centaurea I never planted either. Perhaps they sneaked in with a load of home-made compost, another great 'mixer'. As for the packet of red poppy seed I ordered which turned out to be mostly pink, or white with pink edges: I like it even better than red and I save it every year and watch even more beautiful combinations of colours appear as Nature's best mixers (the bees) do their work. So don't pull out any self-sown party crashers until they have flowered. The chances are that the combination will work, and if it doesn't you can perhaps shift your new plants to a better spot.

You will know that your garden is getting truly cottagey, and truly beautiful, when Nature starts planting treasures for you. So weed carefully, and don't pull out unfamiliar plants too hastily. Canny gardeners can create whole new plantings from judicious replanting of self-sown or bird-sown seedlings.

• Recognising time and place. The natural effect in a garden is created by emphasising the seasons, not contradicting them. Spring will be flying blossoms and nodding bulbs, summer shooting spikes and fluttering petals, autumn a fruit-scented dying blaze, winter clean and clear with austere highlights . . . Out-of-season flowers belong indoors or on the verandah, not in the cottage garden proper where their unnaturalness can only disturb. Similarly, cactuses belong in the desert and orchids in the jungle – not the cottage garden. Only plants which naturally occur and thrive in temperate zones look really at home in a style of garden which originated in a temperate zone. The easiest way to make your garden look like it belongs naturally in the landscape is to plant trees and shrubs which are native to your area – but if this is a bit obvious for you then you must make the effort to research the plants which *might* have been native to your spot if Gondwana and Laurasia hadn't gone their separate ways all those millions of years ago.

Once again the advice to keep rank outsiders in special areas close to the house holds good. An agave surrounded by drifts of forget-me-nots or a mixed planting of proteas and columbines will always be ecologically impossible and hence aesthetically disturbing.

Planning your Garden – The Details

You have asked and answered the basic design questions. Now it's time to get down to detail. In specific terms, how do you plan a cottage garden?

First, measure your house and garden with a long tape measure. You will have to do this in sections, and you should divide up the garden according to its existing functions, or the functions you would like it to have – fruit trees, vegetables, flowers, lawn, and so on. With a ruler and a pencil draw the outline of your home and garden to scale on a large sheet of paper. Enlarging photocopiers are an easy way of making your plan bigger when it

What was basically a plain, rather boring wall has been transformed by planting a climbing red rose and adding shutters to a window.

BELOW LEFT:
A finely crafted fence and a vigorous laurel provide delicious Victorian detail in this Naseby garden.
CHRISTINE DANN

BELOW RIGHT:
Architectural features can be enhanced by careful planting. Here Hydrangea petiolaris *emphasises the gothic door and creates a more mysterious entranceway.*

GLOXINIA.

comes to filling in the finer details, and overlaying several sheets of tracing paper is a good way of adding layers of detail to your base plan.

Use dotted lines to mark in the different sections of your garden according to their different functions. If you like, you can give these different areas names which allude to their character or function: for example, Orchard, Sunny Bank, Family Lawn, or Spring Borders. It may seem a little pretentious for a quarter acre, but when you come to design your planting schemes it does help if you have identified each section by its dominant theme or purpose. Mark in paths, driveways, terraces, sheds and other permanent features, and indicate existing trees and shrubs by drawing rough circles which show how much space they take up. If this doesn't come naturally to you, any good garden design book will provide examples of 'bird's eye' view designs which you can copy from. Design books which I have found helpful are listed in the Bibliography.

Now think about the aspect(s) of your garden, the nature of the soil, whether the shelter is adequate, whether existing utilities are properly sited or need changing, how much time and money you have for your garden . . . in other words, all the 'choices' which are imposed on you. Once you have established the inherent limitations of your site (and yourself) and accepted the need to work with them and not against them, then you can start making real choices about what to plant where.

This is where the tug-of-war between the artist and the botanist in you begins. As an artist you know that to create a sense of peace, harmony and unity you cannot litter your canvas with hundreds of busy little details. As a botanist you are fascinated by the profligate world of plants, and want to find a home for each new discovery. Artists and botanists make different mistakes in gardening. For example, the non-botanising artist might 'think pink' but know only about hydrangeas to execute the theme, while the botanist with no eye for composition might subvert the pink theme with a mishmash of plants as ill-assorted as rhodohypoxis and rhododendrons. Reconciling the two tendencies is the essence of successful garden design, but how is it done?

Perhaps the best advice is to decide which is your strong side and work on improving your weak one. If you're an artist, pay more attention to plants; if a botanist, concentrate on colour and form. Artists will find the photographs at the back of this book, and in other plant identification books, useful, and botanists should make a point of reading the work of professional and successful gardener designers like Gertrude Jekyll, Vita Sackville-West, Russell Page, Stephen Lacey and Christopher Lloyd.

Having taken yourself in hand and reached a point of balance between your opposing inclinations, you can now start making life easier for yourself by using your scale plan (enlarged in sections as necessary) and your knowledge of plants and design. You now start marking on your plan what you want to grow where, what new beds or borders you want to develop, and any suggestions for possible new combinations.

An excellent way to make sure all the information about what is possible remains accessible to you is to keep a 'project scrapbook' of some sort – a book or box or file in which you collect everything which is relevant to your project of transforming your ordinary bit of dirt into a piece of Paradise. It can include pictures clipped from magazines, photos you have taken of other gardens, articles from gardening columns, lists of favourite 'must-grow' plants, photocopied pages from gardening books, records of plantings. As you mull over the contents of this collection on a wet winter evening, and flip through the pages of gardening books, gradually solutions to your gardening problems will occur. From the gardening column on 'Plants with Wet Feet', your photographs of the Botanic Gardens' water garden, Beth Chatto's book *The Damp Garden* and a general plant encyclopaedia you can draw up a list of moisture-loving plants that will disguise your bit of swamp and delight your eye. If your project box also includes catalogues from New Zealand's specialist growers you will even be able to plan when and where you will get what you fancy.

Planning in Detail – The Flower Garden

Take your garden section by section, and design planting schemes for each section which are appropriate to the site. In your plantings, follow the basic cottage garden rules, as follows:

- Use hardy plants, mainly perennials.
- Plant in groups, not in rows. In beds and borders Gertrude Jekyll discovered that the best shape for a group was a lozenge shape parallel to the edge of the border, thus:

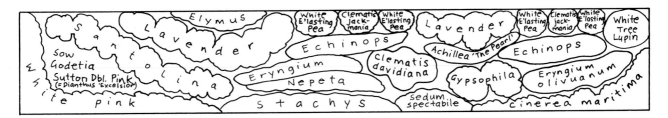

- Use 'natural' materials for paths, seats, mulches, and so on. Shun high-tech metal seating, coloured crazy paving, plastic mulching cloth and the like. They are not traditional, nor organic, so they conflict with the basic ethos of the cottage garden.
- Minimise formal beds and planting schemes. (Exceptions: right next to the house and specially designed herb gardens.)
- Avoid 'fussy' plants, that is plants that require constant staking, clipping, pruning, replanting and other forms of titivation to look right. (Exceptions: fruit trees and bushes; edging plants such as box and lavender.)
- Use plants which echo the environment and plant them so that they imitate/create ecological communities.
- Subordinate structures (house, garage, sheds) to the garden by planting close to the house and using lots of climbing plants, window boxes and collections of plants in pots near doorways.

Even these limitations leave you with a huge choice of plants, so if you want to simplify things still further, restrict your colour schemes. It makes good sense to start by doing this, anyway, until you feel confident to handle the full range of colours. Just as artists do sketches and musicians play exercises, so you can do gardening 'exercises' in the form of draft planting schemes.

First, decide on a colour range – say, pink, white, blue and mauve. Then decide on a height range – say 10 cm to 2 m. Next a space range – say, a border 1 m wide and 10 m long. An aspect – sunny and sheltered. A soil – neutral to alkaline. An 'energy factor' – minimal effort required. Now your personal preferences can come into play, because from the cottage garden 'palette' many solutions to this planting 'problem' are available. Pull out your clippings, gardening manuals and magazines and start dreaming up delicious combinations within that colour range. A solid pink and white backbone to the bed could be provided by old roses – 'Mme Pierre Oger', 'La Reine Victoria' and 'Boule de Neige' are all in the right colour range and are also recurrent and scented. For a feathery effect at the base of the roses, what about love-in-a-mist (*Nigella*), which comes in pink, white and/or blue? Or a blowsy effect with pink and white Shirley poppies? Other alternatives which would give a different impression are blue and/or white cornflowers, or the pale lilac of *Hebe hulkeana*, which has the advantage of staying glossy green all year. For edging the bed, what about the mauve of catmint? Or lavender? Or pinks, parahebes, pansies, campanulas? . . .

From the plants shown in this book alone you could come up with hundreds of potentially pleasing groupings, and it is worth spending a winter evening dreaming up schemes with pencil and paper so that when spring comes you have some good designs ready to get on with. (Some people think this is the best part of gardening – imaginary schemes are always perfect and untroubled by greenfly, slugs or drought!) And if you run out of ideas for design with flowers, why not take up the challenge of a beautiful vegetable garden.

Planning in Detail – The Vegetable Garden

If the modern cottage vegetable garden is not all cabbages and turnips but rather a place where 'anything grows', how do you begin creating especially 'cottage' designs or layouts for the vegetable garden?

Where space is limited, the cottage gardener has no qualms about growing vegetables in front as well as behind the house. Nineteenth-century photographs testify that this was not uncommon in the early days of Pakeha settlement in New Zealand. Here the vegetables are usually grown in straight rows in beds which might be edged with fruit bushes (currants, raspberries, gooseberries), herbs and/or flowering plants, including bulbs and roses. Rose bushes growing alongside the path leading to the front door, with cabbages, lettuces and potatoes in rows at right angles to the roses, may look strange to us now, but it is debatable whether the twentieth-century front garden, with its inevitable patch of lawn dotted with clichéd shrubs and beds of stiff little annuals is more truly ornamental. And why does there seem to be an unspoken rule that fruit trees must be grown behind the house? Citrus trees seem to be the only ones exempt from this rule, perhaps because they seem a little exotic. Yet deciduous fruit trees have beautiful blossom, and ripening fruit always looks lovely.

The corrugated iron tells us it is a pioneer New Zealand cottage, but the garden is pure English. This is Peat Cottage at Ballarat Creek.

B. MACNICOL COLLECTION

If the usual range of fruit trees still seems a little 'common' in the front garden, try choosing one of our numerous more unusual fruits: loquats, guavas, macadamias, olives, bananas, persimmons and mountain pawpaws in the warmer districts; crab apples, rowans, quinces, walnuts, hazelnuts and sour cherries in cooler parts. Beautiful when in fruit, these trees are still attractive without, and they make a living statement that use and beauty are not contradictions in terms.

New Zealand gardeners waste space in a way which must seem sinful to people from more crowded countries, and it would be a good thing if Asian and Pacific immigrants showed New Zealanders of British descent how to make maximum productive use of the whole garden rather than being shamed into conformity with the dominant style.

When all the vegetables are relegated to the back of the house, the usual practice is to grow them in widely spaced straight rows in one large plot of soil. This makes the use of garden machines like rotary hoes more practical, reduces the need for hand weeding, and simplifies the application of powdered fertilisers. It is a style copied from large market gardens and is designed to produce maximum produce with minimum effort. However, it is not the most efficient way to use a small piece of land. It is possible to grow more plants, and minimise digging and weeding, if plants are grown closely together in small deep beds, in what is sometimes called the French or Chinese style of intensive gardening. This style is more aesthetically pleasing and its emphasis on soil feeding and conservation is ecologically sound.

63

While the 'mini-market garden' look is an authentic New Zealand cottage garden style, contemporary cottagers will probably derive more pleasure and produce from their vege gardens if they adopt the French 'potager' style. This style also has an English history, having been pioneered by monastic gardeners in medieval times and adopted by Elizabethan gardeners.

The essence of this style is the multiplication of small square or rectangular beds with paths between them. Land which is lost to pathways is compensated for by the soil in the beds being deeper, richer and less subject to disturbance than the soil in a large plot, and plants are spaced more closely together so that their foliage touches. The shade from their leaves helps retain moisture and discourage weeds. Maintaining the soil pH and fertility required for particular plants, and practising the correct rotation of crops, is also much easier when using separate beds rather than long rows. Plants grown in this way may be slightly smaller than plants grown widely spaced, but as there is no correlation between size, nutritional value and flavour, there is no real loss in quality.

A potager suited to your particular site is easy and fun to design. Like any design based on geometric units, it can be as simple or as grand as you please. The illustration opposite shows a potager in ground plan to give you an idea of how to proceed, and photographs of existing and successful English potagers can be found in Roy Strong's *Creating Small Gardens* and Penelope Hobhouse's *Garden Style*.

If you come to see the potential of vegetable gardening to pleasure the eye as well as the palate, here are some suggestions on ways to transform your boring back yard into a visual feast:

• Runner beans, when first introduced to Europe, were grown for their flowers and not their fruit. The scarlet flowers make a great splash of colour in a predominantly green garden, as do the purple pods of some varieties like 'Purple Knight'. Beans can be grown up trellises, adding height and perhaps shelter to the garden, and providing a framework which looks good all year round.

• Sweet corn too can be used to add height to what is an otherwise flat garden. Corn should be planted in close rows for pollination and support purposes, and although the vege garden is not a *bona fide* play space, small children can derive a very pleasurable 'thicket' experience from rustling through close rows of corn: perhaps this could be tolerated after the cobs have been harvested. Coloured corn cobs are not much good for eating, but delightful for dried decorations, and you can even grow your own pop corn.

• Globe artichokes also add height, and are such visually dramatic plants that even if you fancy the green chokes (and most New Zealanders have yet to acquire the taste) it seems a pity to harvest them. They are also perennials, so can be used to provide permanent accents in the garden.

• Jerusalem artichokes are another plant with very tall stalks, and with leaves that seem to promise sunflowers, but all their productive activity is going on underground. I myself prefer to grow real sunflowers, as the flowers are so impressive, and I would rather feed their seeds to birds than eat Jerusalem artichokes. *Chacune a son goût . . .*

OPPOSITE:
The Kiwi potager in December.

64

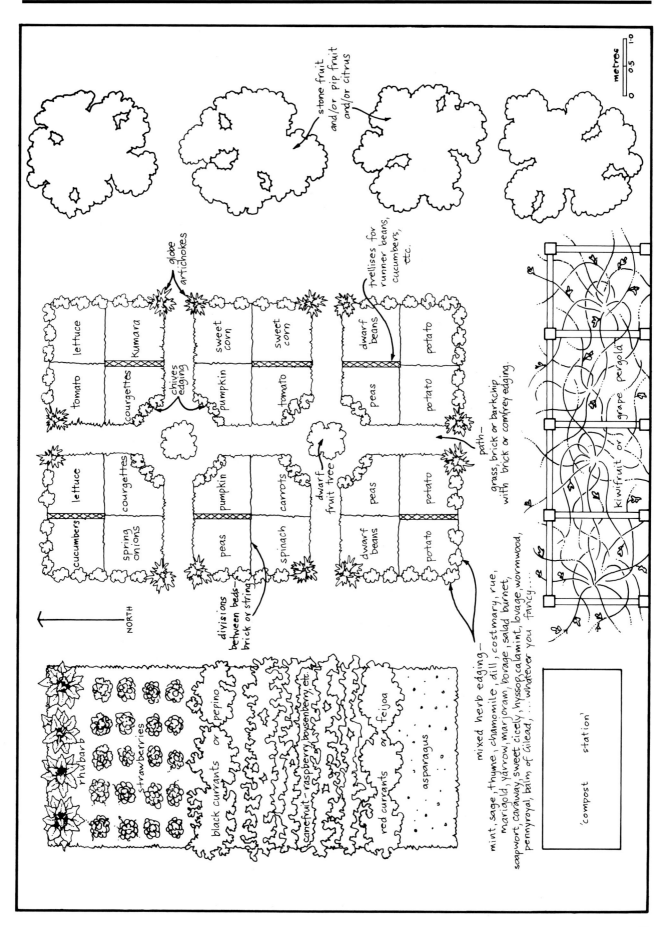

stone fruit and/or pip fruit and/or citrus

metres 0 0.5 1.0

globe artichokes

trellises for runner beans, cucumbers, etc.

lettuce | Kumara

tomato | courgettes

chives edging

sweet corn

sweet corn

pumpkin | tomato

dwarf beans

peas

potato

potato

path—
grass, brick or barkchip
with brick or comfrey edging

NORTH

lettuce | courgettes

cucumbers | spring onions

pumpkin

peas

carrots | spinach

dwarf fruit tree

peas

potato

dwarf beans | potato

divisions between beds—
brick or string

mixed herb edging—
mint, sage, thyme, chamomile, dill, costmary, rue,
marigold, yarrow, marjoram, borage, salad burnet,
soapwort, caraway, sweet cicely, hyssop, calamint, lovage, wormwood,
pennyroyal, balm of Gilead,...whatever you fancy...

kiwifruit or grape pergola

rhubarb

strawberries

black currants or pepino

canefruit—raspberry, boysenberry, etc.

red currants or feijoa

asparagus

'compost station'

65

This garden at Old Salem, USA, gives an idea of what cottage gardens looked like more than 200 years ago. It features herbs in symmetrical plots.
OLD SALEM

• Lettuces (have you noticed?) are no longer just frilly green soccer balls. The smaller green 'buttercrunch' types are better suited to one- or two-person households – one plant per meal and no wastage. They are also preferable for American- or European-style salads. Then there are the 'oak leaf' lettuces, lettuces with red and purple leaves, and frilly little plants of 'lamb's lettuce' (also known as corn salad). Patches of lettuce can now be a picture in their own right. 'Valmine Cos', 'Buttercrunch', 'Royal Oak Leaf', 'Red Salad Bowl', 'Lollo Rosso', 'Red Sails', 'Merveille de Quartre Saisons' and 'Bronze Mignonette' are all available from New Zealand seed suppliers.

• Plants which creep, crawl and spread (cucumbers, pumpkins, kumara) can be encouraged to climb up strings, stakes, chicken wire or trellises and provide another change of level in the vege garden.

• Broad beans are encouraging plants for arriving so early in spring, and their light green leaves and black and white flowers make a handsome contrast to the dark cabbages and silverbeet which have hung on through the winter. However, this is one plant which must be grown in long rows, not clumps, for ease of staking and picking – don't follow the 'square' rule slavishly when it is silly to do so.

• Pot marigolds (*Calendula* spp.), borage and nasturtiums have edible flowers, and bees love borage. A few plants placed randomly will relieve the dominant green and brighten up the vege garden. Don't think of them as stealing soil nutrients from 'real' vegetables, for they can act as traps for some pests and diseases, and by attracting bees they improve pollination.

Further, by making the garden more attractive to the gardener, they encourage her or him to spend more time there, giving the 'real' veges what they need.

• Rhubarb is usually planted in solitary clumps, but if planted in a row it makes an excellent and perennial 'divider' plant between one part of the garden and the next. Similarly, bush, cane or climbing fruits (currants, raspberries, boysenberries, pepinos, gooseberries, Cape gooseberries, kiwifruit) can be used to separate out different parts of the garden, but care must be taken to ensure that they can be easily fertilised and are not being robbed of care or nutrients by veges growing nearby.

Books on vegetable gardening (see Bibliography) will provide detailed information on the cultural requirements of your vegetables, but don't be depressed by the tedium of the 'mini-market garden' model which most of them seem to offer as *the* style of vege gardening. Every cottage-style vege garden will look different because it will be built up from four very variable elements – the basic design, the local soil and climate, the gardener's culinary preferences, and the cultivation requirements of the preferred vegetables. If you use your imagination you can have a vege garden which is a treat to the eye and a pleasure to work in.

Planning in Detail – The Herb Garden

Many a modern cottage garden was begun with a planting of classic herbs on the most unpromising of sites, as Vivienne Plumb can testify:

We bought an old house in the inner city. The backyard was a wee pocket-sized patch full of old man's beard, morning glory, old boots, glass, rubbish, rubbish *and* rubbish . . . For the first summer just one little herb garden about two and a half metres square was planted in a built-up corner, and flowered and flourished vigorously for months. It aroused comments from neighbours on both sides who mainly have seven different types of grass in their back yard! Now the whole back yard has been worked on, and veges, flowers and herbs abound. The size of our back garden is roughly eight by five metres. Herbs look wonderful in it as their small bright-coloured flowers make a pastiche of colour. On the other side of the garden I've planted fragrant flowers – lavenders, pinks, santolina, pineapple sage, thymes and many scented pelargoniums. Around a little seat is chamomile and there are camphor plants, wallflowers and bergamot, and bees go crazy in the wall germander. It's a little oasis.

Whether herbs are given a specially designed area of their own or are incorporated in the garden in other ways will depend on the interests of the gardener. Either way, they are an essential cottage feature. But which herbs are best for cottage gardens and what are the best ways to grow them?

The first herbs to be planted in New Zealand cottage gardens are the *culinary* herbs – parsley, mint, sage, thyme, dill, fennel, chives, chervil, tarragon, basil, angelica, bay, coriander, lemon balm, marjoram, rosemary, savory, sorrel, lovage and sweet cicely.

A prime rule for culinary herb growing is to site the plants near the kitchen. You will resort to dried herbs in cooking if you have to put on gumboots and trek through the rain to pick fresh ones. If you can't site your main herb garden close to the kitchen, grow your favourite herbs in large pots by the door to save you from getting wet on rainy days. These will look very 'cottagey' – so long as you remember to water the pots regularly and keep the herbs green (I speak from desiccated experience). Alternatively, if you have flower beds near the door, feel free to plant herbs among the flowers. Their leaves, which come in every shade of green, gold and purple, provide an excellent foil for flowers.

Culinary herbs can also be grown among the vegetables. Use them to fill in spare patches of ground, or as a border to vegetable beds. Borders of chives, lavender, hyssop and other 'clumpy' flowering herbs look very decorative, while a border of comfrey effectively raises the vegetable bed, preventing mulches from spilling over on to pathways. You can't have too much of this most nutritious herb, whether for compost or for fowl food, and this is a most effective way to grow it.

Medicinal and *scented* herbs can also be grown among the flowers and vegetables, or in pots, but once your herb collection has exceeded twenty different varieties and shows no signs of stopping, you may be looking at putting in a specially designed herb garden. What are the options?

Herb gardens have traditionally had formal designs – neat pathways between geometric beds. Such designs are easy to maintain, and functional, and have a consequent modest beauty. For a small piece of ground, a favourite design seen in herb books is a cartwheel sunk in the ground, with different herbs growing in the spaces between the spokes. It looks very decorative, but where city folk get such things these days I have no idea. The old Elizabethan knot garden, where herbs are planted in the spaces of an elaborate geometric pattern outlined in box or in clippable herbs such as lavender, santolina or rosemary, still has some (energetic) fans, and why not? Others may dream of a herb garden enclosed by brick or stone walls which trap heat and intensify the fragrance of the herbs, and those of us with the right site and ample resources may even achieve such a lovely thing.

However, it seems that the traditional cottage garden, both here and in England, did not have a separate herb garden. Herbs were welcome everywhere, and there are sound reasons for this. Most herbs are 'double-duty' plants. Thyme, chamomile and certain mints can be used as lawns in light traffic areas, or between paving stones. No mowing needed, and much more fragrant than grass. Several of the strongly aromatic herbs are offensive to insects, and most organic gardeners are familiar with 'companion planting' – siting close together plants which complement and protect each other (see pp. 95–6). Herbs which do this job include tansy, feverfew, wormwood, marigold, hyssop and pennyroyal. Tree- and shrub-sized herbs can be incorporated into the overall garden – lavender as a low hedge, prostrate rosemary to spill over a wall, lemon verbena in a shrubbery, bay in a tub with flowers at its feet. Lots of herbs with culinary and medicinal uses are ornamental: yarrow, marigold, hyssop, poppy, catmint, ladies' mantle, meadowsweet, fennel, dill, rue, bergamot, angelica, curry plant, southernwood, scented pelargoniums. All the variegated herbs can be planted in quantity as drifts, clumps or edgings, to enhance the ornamental garden and give it an Elizabethan air.

When planting your garden, allow for interesting or unexpected features. Here an old wooden gate in a hedge creates a new vista.

Don't forget, too, the possibility of creating a truly unique New Zealand herb garden by incorporating some of the native herbs described in the next chapter.

Some excellent herb books are listed in the Bibliography, so if the 'herb bug' bites you badly you can look to these for suggestions on branching out into lots of fascinating directions. Possibilities include herbs for drying, herbs for tisanes (teas), herbs for baths, herbs for perfume . . . Whichever way you go, you will find that herbs are a quick and inexpensive way to give your garden that cottage garden feeling.

Budgeting for a Cottage Garden

You may be bursting with imagination but short of cash. Cottage gardens were traditionally made to a limited budget, so if you're not rich you need not despair. Rich people will be able to create a cottage garden from scratch faster than poor people, but what they create won't necessarily be better than a garden created slowly but surely.

Gardening is a hobby for most people, and like all hobbies you should decide what percentage of your total income you can afford to devote to it. (If you are gardening for food, then garden expenses may come out of your essential expenditure instead. But until you get good at vege and fruit gardening, it is probably better to treat it as a hobby.) If you are an average wage earner, or a superannuitant, you will be lucky to have $10 a week to devote to your garden. On 1990 prices, a bag of compost costs about $5, a shrub $5 to $15, a punnet of vege plants or annuals $3, and a herb plant $3 to $4 . . . Now you know why cottage gardening is do-it-yourself gardening. You are going to need some budgeting strategies and some transition tricks.

The main budgeting strategy is to set priorities. Food for the plants comes first, so the more you can make or scrounge for yourself, the more money you will have to spare for 'luxuries' like plants. Make your own compost, save lawn clippings, fallen leaves and other garden waste, scour beaches for seaweed (*Macrocystis* or bladder kelp is best) and the countryside for animal manure and agricultural byproducts such as straw.

Shelter is another priority. Few things grow well in wind, so if your section is exposed to the elements windbreak plantings or fences have first call on your cash. Other permanent structures or plantings come next – feature trees and shrubs, fruit trees, compost bins, fowl house. Concentrate on the facilities you need to do the job properly and whatever takes a long time to grow.

Only then is it time for the point of the cottage garden – veges, herbs and flowers. The budget gardener is now ready to experience the joys of propagating her own plants, details of which are given in Chapter 7.

Whether you make yourself a step-by-step budget according to your priorities, or whether you just play it by ear, it can be helpful to keep a garden book which contains your plans and ideas, a record of spending, culture requirement notes, a planting record and perhaps a diary. A large spring-clip folder which can be divided into sections is ideal for this purpose. Or you could buy the Yates *Two Year Garden Diary* which is designed for keeping records, and also has room for memos, a site plan, notes, and gives advice on what to plant when.

Record keeping for a cottage garden is certainly neither compulsory nor traditional. The only record keeping which is really important is for vegetable planting so that proper crop rotations can be observed. Details on how to do this are given in Chapter 7. However, if you do want to note down how your garden grows, you will be providing yourself with a valuable record on which to base future planting decisions, and producing an aid to memory which may be pleasurable and useful in later years.

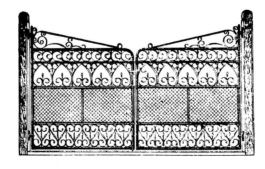

With new materials adapted to old styles, the colonial cottager could opt for ironwork over traditional wood products.
ALEXANDER TURNBULL LIBRARY

Chapter 6

NEW ZEALAND COTTAGE PLANTS

Despite all efforts to turn it into a 'little England', New Zealand retains a character of its own. The rocks, the landforms, the soils, the climate and the native flora and fauna are all distinctive and different. Although derived from British traditions or influenced by British styles via books and magazines, New Zealand gardens are not British gardens and it is foolish to try to imitate styles developed to suit a different climate and way of life. New Zealand cottage gardens have always grown and should always grow the plants best suited to our local conditions. These include our native plants, most of which are evergreen and very un-English.

This does not mean that we have to reject the 'best of British'. It is simply a matter of finding native plants which look comfortable in the cottage context. Most books on gardening with New Zealand natives have so far focused on growing natives either as patches of bush or as alpine rockeries to replicate their natural style of growth, or on blending them into the suburban scene simply as a source of evergreen foliage. There has been no systematic exploration of 'cottage connections' – native plants which are especially suited to cottage-style gardens.

This chapter starts to redress this situation by looking briefly at the traditional British cottage spectrum of flowers, then by making specific recommendations for natives which would be appropriate and attractive in the herbaceous border, the flower beds and the perimeter or specimen plantings of the Kiwi cottage garden. There are also some suggestions for native New Zealand herbs and non-traditional vegetables. Appendices I–IV provide comprehensive lists of plants for the Kiwi cottage garden, arranged into 'Traditional English', 'Cottagey Newcomers', 'New Zealand Cottage' and 'Cottage Roses' categories, so that you can create a mix-and-match garden from this wide range of alternatives.

The Ornamental Garden

The first cottage gardeners planted flowers mainly because they were useful for flavouring food, making medicines or scenting air, clothes and bodies.

*A florists' feast, c. 1760.
Some of the flowers created
by the old florists, like
Dianthus 'Batts Double Red'
and Aquilegia 'Norah
Barlow', continue to flourish.*

But a love of flowers for their own sake soon began to emerge, and culminated in the 'florist' clubs of the eighteenth and nineteenth centuries in which artisans and labourers with limited land would go to extraordinary lengths to raise perfect and enormously varied specimens from a limited range of flowers suited to formal display. Cottage gardeners collected appropriate leftovers from this movement, and from the grand gardens, while still remaining true to some very old-fashioned plants.

Since cottage gardeners of past centuries were not rich enough, or educated enough, to be influenced by fashion in gardening, the basic cottage plant stock varied little and changed slowly. The surplus cash available to the middle classes of the nineteenth century was usually not accompanied (then as now) by an equal excess of taste, and it was to cottages that garden designers reacting against Victorian grossness turned for further inspiration.

Here they found flowering plants which had withstood every test. They were hardy, able to survive in frost and snow. They were mainly perennial or, if annual, they self-sowed freely – most cottage gardeners did not have the time or money to raise or buy bedding plants. They were in a 'refined' colour range – cottage gardeners were on the whole too conservative, too busy, or too fastidious to buy, breed or nurture the flauntingly bright flowers which gained popularity in public bedding schemes and bourgeois gardens in the nineteenth century. They were frequently as useful as well as beautiful, even if by the late nineteenth century they were mainly used as cut flowers for the church or home. They had not sacrificed scent for size or colour. They were not difficult to cultivate. They were rich in historical and literary associations. They were easily propagated by cuttings, division or home-saved seed and this gave them one final, charming attribute: they were plants which were exchanged by friends and neighbours as gifts, bypassing the conformity and expense of the market.

All these historical principles of cottage plant selection are highly relevant to the Kiwi cottage garden today. They dictate the basis of our imported plant stock – the violets, lilies, roses, lavender, columbines, poppies, stocks, pinks, marigolds, larkspur, honeysuckle, sweet peas, wallflowers and so on which have been photographed for this book and are listed in the Appendices. They are also the principles we need to refer to in choosing new plants for cottage gardens.

Since the nineteenth century the traditional cottage garden flowers have been joined by numerous newcomers which fulfil the basic cottage criteria of *hardiness, usefulness, ease of cultivation, refinement* and *exchangeability*. So the first question would-be growers of cottage garden flowers have to ask themselves is: just how purist am I going to be? Do I want to stick to traditional species only? Or (super-purist) traditional varieties only?

If you go down this path, there are certain design themes you can follow – an Elizabethan knot garden, for instance, or a Shakespearean garden. For the average New Zealand cottage gardener, however, such schemes are probably somewhat precious. While eager to rescue old varieties from oblivion and conserve them, the cottage gardener would be violating the spirit of tradition if she did not incorporate appropriate newcomers.

Take the delicate-looking but tough little parahebes, the bold blue Chatham Island forget-me-not (*Myosotidium hortensia*) and our native *Hibiscus trionum* whose flowers are reminiscent of European members of the 'cottage' family Malvaceae. If these plants had been native to Great Britain and not New Zealand they would surely have found their way into cottage gardens. So admit such non-traditional plants into your Kiwi cottage garden, and reject them only if they fail to pass the test which traditional cottage flowers all passed with distinction centuries ago.

Even if you stick to English traditional plants alone, there are still several hundred species and countless varieties to choose from – too many for the average quarter acre. So you must decide on your personal priorities.

Scent? Then go for old roses, pinks, lavender, honeysuckle, jasmine, wallflower, sweet peas, sweet rocket, stock, hyacinth, lilies, violet, or the natives mahoe, toropapa, makomako, tarata, akiraho, raupeka (the Easter orchid), kaikomako, ti kouka . . .

Bright colours? Poppy, paeony, geranium, ranunculas, golden rod, nasturtium, phlox, lavatera, lychnis, helichrysum, valerian, crocosmia, hollyhock, kingcup, sunflower, or the native kakabeak, Chatham Island forget-me-not, poroporo, pohutukawa, rata, yellow daisies and buttercups.

Delicate colours? Foxglove, hellebore, aquilegia, astrantia, campanula, dicentra, narcissus, tobacco flower, love-in-a-mist, Jacob's ladder, Pasque

73

flower, forget-me-not, or *Geranium traversii*, snowberries, native bluebells, hebes, parahebes, mikoikoi . . .

Interesting foliage? Corydalis, lungwort, yarrow, acanthus, angelica, lamium, pelargonium, meadow rue, sweet woodruff, ladies' mantle, or wild Spaniard, celmisias, edelweiss, neinei, toetoe, flax, astelias, pachystegia . . .

Flower arrangements? Pot-pourri? Preserves? Dried flowers? Whatever your needs, there are cottage garden flowers willing and able to meet them. This includes the cottagey natives, which are covered in more detail next.

Cottagey Natives

Incorporating New Zealand native plants into a cottage garden style offers us a wonderful opportunity to create unique gardens which combine the best of both hemispheres. Up till now gardeners focusing on native plants have tended to have a botanical bent, while horticulturists have opted for the variety of bright exotics available. Most of the cottage gardeners I interviewed were busy breaking down this old division, and were enthusiastic about the role New Zealand natives can play not just in providing shelter, year-round greenery, bird 'hotels' and national character, but also in enhancing the garden with flowers, foliage, scent and structure.

So where do we start? There are over twenty genera with New Zealand representatives which contain herbaceous species easily assimilated into cottage-style plantings. Some of them are striking plants with no European equivalents, and need no parochial justifications for their presence in your garden. Others are local variants on well-known themes which you may prefer to grow just for the sense of closer connection.

One of the biggest plant families in the world is the daisy family (Compositae), and New Zealand is famous for its tree and shrub daisies, which are a far cry from the common lawn daisy which is the bane of the turf-proud gardener. In New Zealand the outsize daisies are represented first by a wealth of shrub-sized senecios (many of which have now been placed in the *Brachyglottis* genus), whose leaves have delicately furred, silvery undersides and which remain attractive all year round, and second by an equally large selection of olearias, some of them scented. Especially attractive in full bloom, some of the most desirable olearias and senecios carry their flowers in great balls of blossom, usually white, but sometimes yellow. The *Celmisia* genus is closer to the European idea of a daisy, having single flowers with yellow centres shining up from a circlet of leaves. But the flowers are much bigger and the leaves are silvery, furry and stiff, as befits plants adapted to survive in harsh alpine conditions. My personal daisy favourite is the Marlborough rock daisy, *Pachystegia insignis*, a bold and handsome shrubby daisy – a *dramatic* daisy – which shouts 'Sunshine!' at any gardener who has seen it growing wild in dry and sunny Marlborough, where it billows out of impossible rock crevices. If your cottage garden includes a dry and/or rocky area, some New Zealand daisies are a must, and you will find that the native *Helichrysum bellidiodes* will do just as well as other mat-forming 'everlasting' daisies. So will the attractive little puatea (*Gnaphalium keriense*), which likes to keep its roots cool under rocks. These last two make delicate dried flowers.

Two of New Zealand's bush daisies suitable for cottage gardens. Left, Senecio huntii; *right,* Olearia angustifolia.
OLAF JOHN

Another genus with some uncouth foreign representatives is *Ranunculus.* As you curse the weedy buttercups which infest your garden, you may not be aware that one of New Zealand's most lovely natives, the Mt Cook lily (*Ranunculus lyallii*), is actually a buttercup. Not a plant for hot, dry gardens, of course, but perhaps a challenge which more southern gardeners could take up? *Ranunculus insignis*, unlike the white *R. lyallii*, is a familiar buttercup yellow, but its leaves and flowers are much more glossy and beautiful than those of its northern cousins.

Harakeke or flax (*Phormium tenax*) is a quintessential New Zealand plant which has been eagerly received by foreign gardeners. Many attractive coloured cultivars are available and these can form a nice framing for borders or (for smaller cultivars) a permanent feature in a border. But it would probably be closer to the spirit of cottage self-sufficiency to grow the species as a hedge or windbreak and to seek out the varieties which are best suited to weaving kete (baskets) and korowai (cloaks). Serious weavers and students of botany may like to consult the DSIR Botany Division stations at Havelock North and Lincoln which are now growing collections of over fifty Maori flax varieties suitable for weaving.

Two other desirable plants with the sword-like leaves of flax are the Poor Knights lily (*Xeronema callistemon*), the bold red of its flower stalks playing against their graceful drooping habit, and turutu (*Dianella nigra*) whose deep iridescent blue berries, dripping daintily from long fragile stalks, surely deserve more attention from gardeners who savour delicacy. The New Zealand iris or mikoikoi (*Libertia* spp.) is another delicate plant, its fierce little green or bronze dagger-like leaves belying the dainty white flowers and rich crop of orange berries it carries. Planted in groups, mikoikoi look espe-

*The Mount Cook lily
(Ranunculus lyallii) heralds
summer on an alpine herb
field.*
JOHN CHRISTIE

cially effective when flowering or fruiting. A final native with strappy leaves but graceful white flowers is the rengarenga or Mabel Island lily (*Arthropodium cirratum*) which looks very effective naturalised under deciduous trees. It flowers in early summer and could be an ideal follow-on from late bulbs. It has a 'baby sister', *A. candidum*, a delightful little plant which is better suited to the front of a bed.

As already mentioned, a glorious flower which thrives in the dappled shade beneath trees is the Chatham Island forget-me-not, *Myosotidium hortensia* (pictured p. 36). Seed is readily available and easy to grow, and the plant also seeds itself freely in damp, rich soil. Anyone who has seen the drifts of these bold blue flowers, highlighted with white, growing beneath the trees at the Otari Native Plant Museum in Wellington, would surely be inspired to grow them if they had the right conditions. For size and colour they are probably New Zealand's most dramatic flower, and deserve to be much better known. New Zealand has more humble forget-me-nots too, and you may like to try species such as *Myosotis explanata*, *M. macrantha* and *M. australis*, which are white or yellow, and much more solid both in leaf and flower than the blue European forget-me-not, *M. sylvatica*. *Myosotis explanata*, the Arthur's Pass forget-me-not, is a superb choice for edging white gardens, its white flowers clustering on top of a neat clump of evergreen leaves with silvery-grey highlights.

New Zealand gentians (*Gentiana* spp.), like New Zealand forget-me-nots, are white rather than blue, and merit more attention. The New Zealand harebell (*Wahlenbergia* spp.), in white or blue, is our southern hemisphere equivalent of the *Campanula* genus. It is one of New Zealand's prettiest wild flowers, and can be seen growing readily on tussocky hills.

Ourisia macrophylla.
OLAF JOHN

The different species of *Ourisia*, with lopsided white flowers (two petals up, three down), brighten up damp and shady places in mountainous areas throughout New Zealand and will do the same in cool, damp gardens. The New Zealand eyebright (*Euphrasia cuneata*) is like an even prettier ourisia, with a gold and purple throat and dented petals. Another small white flower with gold and purple streaks at its throat, which also favours damp places, is the native violet, *Viola cunninghamii*. It has no scent, but is quite as attractive as European violets. In my garden it keeps company with *Jovellana sinclairii*, a calceolaria which is far more refined than its garish cultivated cousins. It is white, keeps its purple spots inside its bell-shaped flowers, and hangs from soft stalks above a clump of mid-green leaves. It is very suitable for the front of a border.

An unusual taller plant for growing in clumps in a border is the native hibiscus, *Hibiscus trionum*. It is a biennial which readily seeds itself, so once you get it going you won't lose it, although it is sensitive to frost and easiest to grow in mild, coastal locations. The yellow flowers with deep purple centres are followed by distinctive seed capsules, making the plant interesting for half the year. The 'Maori onion' (*Bulbinella angustifolia* and *B. hookeri*) is a deeper yellow, and grows on a tall stalk – like a small and attractive cousin of the red hot poker. Bulbinellas would look quite at home near some 'wild Spaniards' (*Aciphylla* spp.). Because of their extremely hard and sharp spines, only enthusiasts tend to grow Spaniards, although their huge flower stalks, smothered in tiny flowers and bristling with spines, are bound to excite comment, and one species (known as taramea) was a staple of the Maori perfume trade. The resemblance to hemlock, or carrots gone to seed, may also prejudice gardeners against the *Anisotome* genus with its characteristic umbel-shaped flowerheads. But if plants like angelica have educated you to see beauty in the Umbelliferae then you may like to try planting some of the native members of this family such as the scented common anisotome, *Anisotome aromatica*.

If geranium to you means a blaze of bright colour on a woody stalk, you will think again when you see how dainty in leaf and colour the native geraniums are. *Geranium microphyllum* and *G. traversii* can easily be grown anywhere a cottage-style geranium with delicate petals and small leaves is preferable to a gaudy, large-leafed pelargonium.

If you like bright pinks and reds, take a look at the latest manuka (*Leptospermum scoparium*) cultivars. There are some very desirable varieties of this scratchy-leafed shrub available, in both single and double forms, with leaf colour ranging from deep green to bronze. I find the double white forms especially attractive – rather like a New Zealand equivalent of the English may bush. Sprigs of dried manuka are ideal for dried flower arrangements, and of course this plant wasn't called the 'tea-tree' for nothing. An infusion of the green leaves of the species makes a mild, slightly astringent green tea – very refreshing for thirsty trampers.

If you have planted members of the foreign *Pieris* genus because you like their hanging, white, bell-shaped flowers in spring, did you know that you can get a reprise on the theme later in the year if you plant the native shrubs *Gaultheria crassa* or *G. colensoi*, which ring on into summer? The common

Just two of New Zealand's wealth of attractive hebes. Left, Hebe odora; *right,* Hebe diosmifolia.

OLAF JOHN

English name for these shrubs is snowberry. Snowy mountains is likewise a suitable association for one of New Zealand's most charming native flowers, the native edelweiss (*Leucogenes grandiceps* and *L. leontopodium*). I am always amazed that our edelweiss looks so like the European one, since our flora so seldom resembles that of Europe. *Linum monogynum*, or rauhuia, a soft, low plant with white flowers, also has a passing resemblance to its blue-flowered European cousin, linen flax or *L. usitatissimum*, though rauhia is probably a prettier garden plant. It also provides potential for teasing visitors by asking them to spot the 'true' flax. *Craspedia uniflora* or woollyhead is another cute and hardy plant to grace a New Zealand garden, having white or yellow flowerheads like tight, round pom-poms.

New Zealand is the *Hebe* capital of the world, but how do you go about choosing between the hundreds of hebes? There are now lots of beautiful cultivars of these versatile shrubs available, some with long purple and pink flowerheads, such as *Hebe* 'Inspiration' and *Hebe* 'Pink Payne', which would look good at the back of borders. Keep an eye out for *Hebe diosmifolia*, which carries a great load of white flowers tinged with lavender, and its cultivars such as *H.* 'Wairau Beauty', and *H.* 'Lilac Gem'.

Hebes come in a variety of shapes and colours, from the tree-sized *H. parviflora*, which looks especially lovely when its slim green leaves are buried in white blossom, to the compact little *H. albicans*, with tiny grey-green leaves and tight white flowers. *H. townsonii* is another one to watch out for, although it is worth remembering that since hebes naturally cover the length and breadth of New Zealand, with species adapted for every niche from shore to mountaintop, you should check that a preferred variety will do well in your area. Hebes can have a very localised range in the wild, and that includes my favourite for cottagey effects, *Hebe hulkeana*, which has unusually soft, wide

Mazus radicans, an attractive groundcover for damp places.
OLAF JOHN

leaves and beautiful drooping sprays of palest lilac flowers (hence the name 'New Zealand lilac'). A final hebe which I think should become a New Zealand cottage classic is *Hebe hartii* (sometimes sold as 'Lavender Spray') which spreads very readily as a ground cover and is covered with pale mauve flowers which bees adore in late spring/early summer.

I have left my favourite 'Kiwi cottager' till last – and I'm glad to see that the parahebes seem to be catching on. These neat little evergreen plants with tiny serrated leaves in a deep, shiny shade of green, and smothered in tiny mauve or white nodding flowers throughout summer and into autumn, are ideal for edgings, for the fronts of borders, for naturalising, or anything else you fancy. They also grow easily from cuttings and I think they are very 'cottagey'.

Native groundcovers

Does New Zealand have anything to compare with enthusiastic ground-covers like creeping Jenny and snow-in-summer, which are traditional to English cottage gardens? In my view, two species are quite as fine as their foreign competitors – *Selliera radicans*, which has prolific white flowers capable of carpeting the ground in the most inhospitable seaside sites, and *Pratia angulata*, which is similarly flowered and favours damp, shady spots. Pratia also has purple berries.

There are other contenders, too. Huge, glossy, purplish-red berries are the chief feature of an unusual native, *Fuchsia procumbens*, which will sprawl over walls or creep over the ground. Horticulturally minded trampers will have admired the shiny little orangey-red berries of the nertera (*Nertera* spp.) which crawls over banks, logs and rocks in the forest to good effect: for damp gardens it would make a most attractive groundcover. Our native cotulas, with their tiny, fern-like leaves, are in demand overseas as ground-covers, as are the smaller species of gunnera, with their toothed leaves. Another plant which will do well in damp corners is the swamp musk, *Mazus radicans*, which has violet-like flowers. If you have a dryish space to

Puawananga (Clematis paniculata) cascades through treetops in spring.
JOHN CHRISTIE

cover, the creeping shrub pinatoro (*Pimelea prostrata*) will reward with tiny glaucous leaves and clusters of white flowers. It seems to like sun – mine died out when it got shaded!

Native climbers

If you like your trees and walls to do double duty by supporting climbers, then New Zealand natives provide some original options. The 'Maori jasmine' (*Parsonsia capsularis* and *P. heterophylla*) has little scent but very attractive creamy-white flowers. Grow it up a deciduous tree which flowers at a different time and you will get two 'blossom times'. Puawananga (*Clematis paniculata*) hangs in forest trees in spring like a cloud of white stars fallen to earth. Give it a cool, damp root run and it will oblige on walls and verandahs too, and look much more refined than the overworked *Clematis montana*. Climbing rata (*Metrosideros* spp.) come in red and white, and make good cover for banks and walls.

If you have somewhere you think is appropriate for a decorative member of the blackberry family, you should think about tataramoa or bush lawyer (*Rubus* spp.). Its prickles (or should I say claws?) are likely to prejudice most people against it, but the leaves (there are green and bronze varieties) are really quite handsome. It is a suitable plant for repelling intruders!

Tecomanthe speciosa is a very choice, yellow-flowered climber, with most attractive large glossy leaves. It has an interesting history of being rescued from the wild when on the brink of extinction and was once regarded as the rarest plant in the world. Finally, for dense glossy green leaves and glowing orange berries, plus a fast growth rate, you can't go past kohia (*Tetrapathea tetrandra*).

Trees and shrubs

With so many distinctive native trees and shrubs to choose from, it is hard to draw up a short 'cottage' list. The following selection focuses only on choice small trees and large shrubs, which will not overpower a small garden. Most of them fulfil the cottage criterion of being double-duty plants.

If your cottage garden needs a hedge, why not choose a vernacular one? Taupata (*Coprosma repens*) and akiraho (*Olearia paniculata*) are fast-growing plants which can be kept as neat, dense hedges with an annual trim. They are evergreen, but not dark and sombre like the traditional English evergreen hedge plants yew and box, and are also very hardy in dry and coastal sites. Some people love the scent of akiraho flowers: they are certainly distinctive, sweet but tangy.

The native pittosporums can also be clipped as hedges. Karo (*Pittosporum crassifolium*) is the species most often treated this way. It makes a big, southerly-buster stopper of a hedge. *P. tenuifolium* (kohuhu) has smaller, shinier leaves and is attractive hedge material. Red beech (*Nothofagus fusca*) and golden totara (*Podocarpus totara* 'Aureus') are too large to let loose as trees in a small garden but they make very impressive and beautiful hedges. For a small, neat hedge use korokio (*Corokia cotoneaster*, *C. x virgata* or *C. buddleioides*). The bronzy forms of korokio make a nice colour alternative for hedging, as does the purple-leaved form of the ake ake, *Dodonea viscosa*. Please note that this ake ake is quite different from the Chatham Island ake ake, *Olearia traversii*, which is the ultimate tough-as-old-boots hedge plant for exposed coastal situations.

For shelter plantings which you don't want to clip into hedge shape, there are plenty of suitable *Olearia* species, the manuka (*Leptospermum scoparium*) and kanuka (*Kunzea ericoides*), the large varieties of *Coprosma*, and the pittosporums. Kotukutuku, the tree fuchsia (*Fuchsia exorticata*), could be grown amidst such a planting for the pleasure of its paper bark and the sweet taste of its black berries, and mahoe (*Melicytus ramiflorus*) deserves a place for producing the best skeleton leaves in the world and one of the most delicious scents. Rangiora (*Brachyglottis repanda*) comes in green- and purple-leaf forms, with silver fuzz on the flip side of the outsized leaves and a froth of cream flowers in late spring. The reddy-brown leaves of horopito (*Pseudowintera colorata*) provide a contrast among green foliage. Hutu (*Ascarina lucida*) has tender green-toothed leaves on black stems, while wharangi (*Melicope ternata*) has leaves of a similar light green which grow in groups of three. The tainui or *Pomaderris* genus have tough-looking leaves but reward with prolific gold or cream flowers, and ramarama (*Lophomyrtus bullata*) has remarkably bumpy and veined leaves. It is now available in several colour variations and popular for flower arrangements.

An effective contrast with the upright trees is the forest cabbage tree, ti ngahere (*Cordyline banksii*), with its drooping flax-like leaves and sprays of sweet-scented white flowers. The mountain cabbage tree or toii (*Cordyline indivisa*) is a wonderfully mop-headed little tree, with very broad, sword-shaped leaves and flowers hanging in thick bunches like bananas. The *Pseudopanax* genus includes the shrubs and trees usually known as 'three finger' and 'five finger', as well as the distinctive lancewood. There is now a

variety of attractive *Pseudopanax* cultivars to choose from, including purple-, gold- and variegated-leaf forms, and they can be used to lift a planting of shrubs.

For specimen trees there is nothing wrong with starting with the old favourite, the kowhai (*Sophora tetraptera*, *S. microphylla*). There is a kowhai for every situation. *S. tetraptera* is ideally suited to an underplanting of spring bulbs, perhaps to tone with or succeed its own golden flowers in early spring. If your garden is small there are the 'Gnome' varieties which are smothered in large flowers at knee height, and I was once lucky enough to find a specimen of *S. longicarinata*, which is a much smaller tree than *S. tetraptera* or *S. microphylla*, with incredibly tiny leaves. Kowhai are easy to grow from seed, which should first be soaked in boiling water or chipped to crack the hard seed coat. But they can spend up to ten years looking like a tangled mess before they display a real trunk – this especially applies to *S. microphylla*.

The pohutukawa (*Metrosideros excelsa*) is another popular tree, and there are now attractive variegated forms of *M. excelsa* and other pohutukawa species available. The pohutukawa has been hammered hard in recent years, and in parts of northern New Zealand there are places where the once common 'New Zealand Christmas tree' is now a rare sight. This beautiful tree is its own best advertisement, and cottage gardeners should join the replanting campaign. Pohutukawa can be grown in large containers, as can the popular kakabeak (*Clianthus puniceus*), which now comes with red, pink or white flowers. The kakabeak is perhaps the closest we come to a Maori 'cottage' plant, as it was planted around some Maori homes in pre-European times. This probably saved it from extinction in the wild, where it is now very rare.

Most New Zealand gardeners know these three natives, but after that their knowledge or their imagination fails and they begin to plant foreign trees for effect. Before you pay big money for a golden ash, magnolia, liquidamber or

*The beautiful flowers of
Hoheria lyallii.*
OLAF JOHN

other specimen tree, consider that for one-third of the cost you could have an equally effective native tree.

The whau (*Entelea arborescens*) has dramatically large leaves, huge bunches of white flowers in spring, and similarly large clusters of prickly burrs (like sweet chestnuts) in autumn. It is also one of the lightest woods in the world. The kaikomako (*Pennantia corymbosa*) puts on a mantle of sweet-scented white flowers in time for Christmas, and provides food for bellbirds (korimako). The putaputaweta (*Carpodetus serratus*) also dresses in white in summer, and has attractively marbled leaves all year round and a distinctive pale trunk. The white trunk of the tarata or lemonwood (*Pittosporum eugenioides*) shows to advantage if it is grown as a specimen. Its long leaves are a glossy green all year round, and the scent from its pale yellow flowers in September is heavenly.

The titoki (*Alectryon excelsum*) is as graceful and as large as the European ash (which it resembles), and has the advantage of being evergreen and carrying bright red and black fruits for months. The hinau (*Elaeocarpus dentatus*) is also a bigger tree, but worth growing for its spring flowers, which are like white bells with the most delicate scalloped edges. The karaka (*Corynocarpus laevigatus*) has its moment of glory in late summer, when its orange fruits glow among its large glossy leaves, and ferment on the ground with a scent of apricots. This tree, which seems to have been the only tree planted specifically for its fruit by the pre-European Maori, should perhaps receive as much attention in the New Zealand cottage garden as the crab apple, elderberry and other imported wild fruits, although the kernel is highly poisonous unless well cooked, so perhaps it is not a good tree for gardens frequented by children. Children will, on the other hand, be quite safe with the wineberry (*Aristotelia serrata*). Its winey-pink flowers in spring have a sweet scent, and its black berries in summer are attractive and edible to both humans and birds. Its distinctive serrated leaf is a clue to its Maori name, makomako: mako is the shark, and makomako's leaves look very like green sharks' teeth.

Another delicious scent comes from the cream to crimson flowers of the toropapa (*Alseuosmia macrophylla*), which is worth growing for its fragrance alone. The different species of *Hoheria* or lacebark (and there are now variegated cultivars) all have the pleasing habit of offering prolific white flowers in late summer – a welcome reminder of spring in the dog days. The notable English gardener Vita Sackville-West devoted a column to singing the praises of *Hoheria lyallii*, a valued and (to her) exotic member of her famous garden at Sissinghurst. It is a pity it is not better appreciated in its native land.

If you favour conifers as specimens, the New Zealand cedars (*Libocedrus bidwilli* and *L. plumosa*) will grow into attractive shapes and require far less pruning than the more common foreign conifers. However, one of the most stunning trees for shape is the world's southernmost palm, the nikau (*Rhopalostylis sapida*). It is a strikingly distinctive tree, and I cannot see it without thinking of four Ws – warm, wet, wild and west – for these are the conditions and places in which it loves to grow. What wonderful associations to bring into any garden. For the drier east coast, the common ti kouka or cabbage tree (*Cordyline australis*) is similarly distinctive, with the added

bonus of deliciously scented creamy flowers hanging from its branches in great swags in late spring. It is currently under threat in the wild, so please plant lots more. Both the nikau and the ti can grow (slowly) into impressive single specimens, but I always think they look happier in small groups, and make an unusual and compact form of grove. So think about it, if you have the room.

Finally, what New Zealand cottager could resist the fern family? Some of our earliest European-style cottages were made of fern tree trunks, and a community of ferns, both large and small, on the shady side of a cottage will always look very special and very right in New Zealand. All the tree ferns (*Cyathea* and *Dicksonia* spp.) are hardy plants, and can provide shade and shelter for the smaller ferns. Choose the smaller tree ferns if you have a small house, though – the mamaku (*Cyathea medullaris*) can reach twenty metres, while the ponga (*Cyathea dealbata*) can grow to ten metres.

There are lots of hardy small ferns. Look for members of the *Blechnum* and *Asplenium* genera, *Doodia media*, *Polystichum* spp., *Pteris tremula*, *Lygodium articulatum* and *Adiantum* spp. Some ferns, such as the blechnums, can survive dryish conditions, but the fleshy-leaved kidney ferns and the delicate filmy ferns need lots of water to look their best. For this reason a separate fern house or grove is a good idea if you want to specialise in these plants. Fern tree logs can be used in many attractive ways in a Kiwi cottage garden, but in the interests of forest and fern conservation don't buy fern logs extracted from virgin bush.

The Herb Garden

For a more contemporary and indigenous style of herb garden, the addition of some New Zealand native herbs amongst your traditional favourites is a must.

Suitable for mixing in with the English herbs are hioi, the native mint (*Mentha cunninghamii*), and native members of the Umbelliferae family (to which dill, fennel and parsley belong) such as *Scandia rosifolia* (rose-leaved anise) and *Gingidia montana* (Maori anise), which have recorded medicinal uses. In the same family, but purely ornamental, are members of the similar

Anisotome genus, the 'Kiwi carrots', which are worth growing for their handsome, feathery leaves and attractive umbels of seeds.

Every New Zealand garden should grow some kokihi, or New Zealand spinach (*Tetragonia tetragonioides*), which Captain Cook fed to his sailors to prevent scurvy. Several seed companies offer improved garden varieties of this native vegetable (it also makes an acceptable fleshy-leaved groundcover for shady banks). Enthusiasts for unusual plants will want to grow nau, Cook's scurvy grass (*Lepidium oleraceum*), which is now very rare in the wild (thanks to grazing animals, and not vitamin-deprived eighteenth-century sailors!) and the wild celery (*Apium australe*). The puwha (*Sonchus oleraceus*), although not endemic, is of course New Zealand's best-known 'native' vegetable, with a native cousin, *Sonchus kirkii*. It also has medicinal uses – Christina MacDonald recommends it for keeping wounds clean.

Plantains (*Plantago* spp.) are anathema to most gardeners, but not to a herbalist. The native species, commonly known as kopakopa, are as effective medicinally as the introduced ones.

Last but not least among the tender herbs is kopata or common avens (*Geum urbanum* var. *strictum*). A pretty yellow flower enhances the healing leaves. The piripiri (*Acaena* spp.), that most handsome of 'bidibids', is in favour as a groundcover in rockeries in Britain where it has been bred in several shades. (New Zealand nursery people please note!) It also provided a cure for bladder and kidney complaints.

Most of the Maori herbal remedies come from trees and shrubs rather than herbaceous plants, and there are several common broadleaf evergreens which you should incorporate in your boundary plantings or shrubbery if you want a comprehensive New Zealand herb garden. They include kawakawa (*Macropiper excelsum*), koromiko (*Hebe salicifolia*), manono (*Coprosma grandifolia* and *C. robusta*), rangiora (*Brachyglottis repanda*), horopito (*Pseudowintera colorata*), kumerahou (*Pomaderris kumerahou*), and of course harakeke or New Zealand flax (*Phormium tenax*).

For further information on New Zealand herbs and herbal medicines, you can consult Christina MacDonald's *Medicines of the Maori* and Brooker, Cambie and Cooper's *New Zealand Medicinal Plants*. Or perhaps you know a kaumatua who will share this knowledge with you. Whatever the route to learning about the medicinal qualities of our native plants, they are well worth the discovery, and an ideal addition to a garden with indigenous character.

The Vegetable Garden

Vegetables were the *raison d'être*, the heart and soul, of the traditional cottage garden. Growing your own began as a necessity, and was promoted to a virtue by zealous Victorians. These days, when it is not necessary and no longer regarded as virtuous, is growing your own veges still relevant to cottage gardening?

To say no to that question would be to deny the efforts of my parents, grandparents and many more generations of vegetable-gardening ancestors. It would be to deny the sweetness of sitting on the sunny back porch on Christmas morning, shelling (and stealing) fresh new peas grown specially

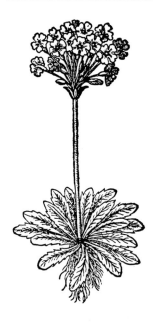

for the Christmas feast. New peas which would snuggle up to tender baby carrots and tiny white potatoes on the good china, all straight from the garden and into the celebration. Yes, a cottage garden must have vegetables. But which vegetables?

It would be very boring to stick to the limited range of vegetables available to the first cottage gardeners. It would also be totally inappropriate for New Zealand gardeners, many of whom garden in sub-tropical conditions and have access to vegetables from right around the Pacific. Within the cottage-style potager described in the previous chapter, the Kiwi cottage gardener should feel free to experiment with fruit and vegetables which are regarded as exotic in England. Vegetables and fruits which are easily grown outdoors in the warmer parts of New Zealand include kumara, oka (yams), taro, pumpkins, melons, capsicums, aubergines (eggplants), tomatoes, feijoas, avocados, tamarillos, kiwifruit, loquats, Cape gooseberries, pepinos and a range of Oriental greens. New Zealand cottage gardens should contain these specialities of the region wherever possible. Gardeners in the cooler parts of New Zealand may have to grow the heat-loving veges under glass, but their open ground need not be dull. Unusual and often superior varieties of vegetables and fruit can be obtained from specialist sources, listed in Chapter 8.

There really *is* nothing like fresh vegetables from your own (organic) garden. It is the easiest way to ensure that your veges are free of the chemical residues, bruises, rotten bits and other ills of shop-bought produce. Nor has there been time for precious vitamins and minerals to be lost through long or incorrect storage. Another advantage of growing your own is that you can concentrate on what you like most, and have a bit of fun with your food. I grow lots of French beans in summer and eat them long before they'd be considered big enough to go to market. As long as a finger and nowhere near as wide, topped and tailed, a few minutes in a minimum of boiling water, a nob of butter and a grinding of black pepper . . . ahh! How beautifully they squeak on the teeth before slipping down the throat. Unusual veges are good value too. Put some purple 'Maori' potatoes among the white ones in your next potato salad and enjoy the suspicious questions of your guests.

Anyone who likes to cook good food will take the art of vegetable gardening seriously, and luckily there are two excellent New Zealand books (*The Cook's Garden* and *More from the Cook's Garden*) already devoted to the soil/stomach interface. Unfortunately vegetable gardening has an undeserved reputation for being boring because it is so obviously useful. I used to suffer from this misconception until I discovered that vege gardens could look just as good as the produce itself tastes – hence the emphasis on the well-designed vege garden in Chapter 5. Now it's a pleasure to get out there and pull those weeds . . .

Be lateral, not literal, in choosing plants for your New Zealand cottage garden. An extensive range of very useful books is available on gardening with New Zealand natives, and the most exciting challenge for cottage gardeners of the future must surely lie in melding the indigenous and exotic elements of our flora into a new style of garden which speaks to our unique experience as inhabitants of a temperate South Pacific isle.

Chapter 7

THE PRACTICE

You have pored over the plant books and catalogues, you have made a list of 432 plants you simply cannot live without – and you have discovered that you can't afford one half of them and don't know how to look after the other half. A little patience, and a little more effort – prime requirements for the successful cottage gardener – and you will have both the plants and the skills.

This chapter covers the basics of how to feed the soil which will feed your plants, how to care for your soil and plants, how to propagate your own plants, what you need to grow to be self-sufficient, and important considerations to bear in mind if growing traditional English cottage plants in New Zealand conditions.

Feeding the Soil

If you want your garden to feed you, you must feed your garden.

Artificial fertilisers are to gardens what takeaway foods are to humans; they support life but they do not nourish. There are many organic manures and fertilisers which will nourish your garden, and every cottage garden worth the name is also fed by compost made on the premises. Organic fertilisers derived from animal sources include horse, sheep, hen and cow manure, bone meal, blood and bone, fish and fish meal. How do you get your hands on this lovely stuff? Your local garden centre is the obvious source of supply, and the better-stocked ones will have a good range of manures and composts. Stock and station agencies which have a garden centre are often economic places to shop – canny farming folk balk at paying high prices for manure. Or you can go into the country and get your own. Horse owners on the outskirts of cities often sell horse manure in bags at the gate. Chicken farms usually sell hen manure (although organic purists will be suspicious of manure from battery farms where chickens are dosed with various drugs). Service clubs and other organisations sometimes sell manure to raise funds – this is usually sheep manure collected from under wool sheds. If you know a sheep farmer, this is a great source of supply. But remember the general rule of thumb not to use animal manures fresh, as they may burn your plants or cause them to grow too fast. Leave them in a heap (covered with sacks or plastic sheeting) to rot down for two to three months.

Animal manures are rich in nitrogen, and the amounts of other key elements vary according to the type of manure (see Table). If you live near a fish factory or go fishing yourself, you may be able to get fish waste or fish meal – nutritious but smelly, so it is best to bury it as soon as it arrives. Blood and bone and bone meal are byproducts of meat works and can be bought in powdered form at garden centres and hardware stores. They are best used as 'boosters' – for example, mixed in with soil in planting holes or sprinkled alongside vegetables.

Vegetable-derived fertilisers include seaweed, comfrey, straw, hay, green manures and, of course, compost. Most New Zealanders live near the coast and can gather seaweed – the best time to do it is on a fine day after a storm has washed up lots of fresh weed. You can put the seaweed in a compost bin, or chop it and put it directly on the garden as a mulch. *Don't* wash it first – the salts on the weed contain potassium which you want in your soil. Choose softer weed – bladder kelp (*Macrocystis*) is good because anything

Major nutrients in organic fertilisers

The approximate nitrogen, potassium and phosphorus content of some common organic materials which may be used directly as fertilisers.

	Percentage composition		
	Nitrogen N	Phosphorus pentoxide P_2O_5	Potassium oxide K_2O
Animal manures			
Horse	0.6 (1.5)	0.2 (0.5)	0.6 (0.4)
Cow	0.6 (0.4)	0.2 (0.2)	0.5 (0.2)
Pig	0.5 (0.5)	0.3 (0.4)	0.5 (0.3)
Sheep	0.9 (0.8)	0.3 (0.4)	0.9 (0.5)
Hen	1.0 (1.4)	0.8 (1.1)	0.5 (0.5)
Other materials			
Basic slag	—	12–20	—
Bone meal	3.5	23	0.2
Blood and bone	6.9	10.6	—
Dried blood	7–14	—	—
Fish meal	5–10	6–14	—
Feathers	8–12	—	—
Leather dust	9.0	1.0	—
Seaweed meal	2.0	0.3	2.7
Wood ash	—	1–10	6–10
Woodstove soot	0.5–6.0	—	—
Urine (human)	6.9	3.2	3.4
Comfrey (wilted)	0.74	0.24	1.19
Sewage sludge	2–3	0.5–1.5	0.1–0.3

Source: *Organic Gardening in New Zealand*, Richard Llewellyn Hudson, p. 49.

Getting ready for the flower show. The florist tradition survives transplantation to a new land, and prize plants are displayed in pots.
ALEXANDER TURNBULL LIBRARY

larger, such as bull kelp, is hard to chop up and takes too long to rot down. How do you chop it? Put it in a pile and slice it with a spade – watch out for your toes!

Comfrey is a highly nutritious plant which organic gardeners grow specifically for fertiliser. Chopped leaves can be used as a mulch, made into liquid manure, added to the compost heap, and fed to animals and fowls. Allocate a sunny patch of the garden for comfrey (which is a long-lived perennial) or use it as an edging for vegetable beds. Feed it well with a nitrogen-rich fertiliser in spring and summer, and harvest the leaves three or four times over spring, summer and autumn.

Hay and straw can be used as mulches and allowed to rot into the soil, but they are high in carbon so you must add some nitrogen-rich fertiliser when preparing the bed for a new crop.

Green manures are plants grown just for cutting down and digging into the soil to increase its organic matter content. They are a superior alternative to leaving the ground empty, as they can add nourishment while preventing weeds from taking over the bare ground. Mustard and ryegrass can be grown as green manures but legumes such as lucerne and lupin are better as they fix nitrogen in the soil. You must dig the crop in while it is still soft and green – do not let it flower or grow woody. An alternative to digging it all in is to cut it down, put the tops in the compost, and dig the roots in. Even in the cooler parts of New Zealand green manures are a practical crop over winter. Planted in the autumn, they will start to grow again in August or September and can be chopped up and dug in in good time for the traditional

Labour Weekend planting of main crop seeds. A New Zealand cottage vegetable garden should be more green than brown to look at all year, even in mid-winter Southland, and if you have been a bit slack or inaccurate in planning your succession of vegetables, green manures will improve your outlook as well as your soil.

Seaweed, comfrey, straw and green manures are all valuable vegetable-derived fertilisers, but the ultimate organic fertiliser is of course compost. Superior compost is a rich, warm, black, sweet-smelling, soft, friable substance which looks good enough to eat without the bother of passing it through vegetables! To make compost of this quality requires careful attention, and for most practical purposes something less than perfection will suffice. However, the novice compost maker is probably wondering how to advance beyond a gluggy, lumpy mixture in which slimy, smelly, half-rotted peelings and hard unrelenting stalks are still far too much in evidence.

Advice on how to make good compost is freely available in many gardening books and periodicals. It is worth reading at least two views on the subject and making sure you understand the principles, and then work on finding a system that suits you. Some people are perfectly happy to put up makeshift chicken-wire enclosures, fill them with compostable materials and leave them to get on with it. This is a slow but sure method. Others will want to get faster results, and after several years of experiment to find the balance between minimum energy expenditure and maximum compost output I use the following system, which produces passable compost in a reasonably short time.

The first essential for compost making on the cottage garden scale is bins. You will need at least three bins – 1 m × 1 m × 1 m is an ideal size. The bins should be in a row, so that you can shift compost from one bin to the next. The bins can be made of timber, wire, old iron, or whatever you please, but they should have:

- holes in all sides (gaps between slats of wood, holes punched in iron, etc);
- a removable front.

Why? First answer – because compost is formed by aerobic decomposition. Aerobic means air, and if you don't let air into your compost bin you will retard decomposition. Sophisticated bins have raised and slatted bottoms so that air can get in underneath – the same principle as a fire grate. Second answer – it is much easier to get compost out of a bin with a removable front than to have to lift it over a metre each time you remove a shovelful.

Compost bins should be sited in a warm part of the garden (heat hastens decomposition), preferably close to the vege garden, which will use most of the compost. Naturally you will want to use the warmest part of your garden for growing choice fruit and vegetables or for sunbathing, so some compromise will be necessary here. The point is made so that you think about your compost requirements early, and don't bung the bins in a cold, dark corner as an afterthought.

To keep in the heat, and keep out the rain, a cover for the bins is desirable. Black polythene sheet, cut a little larger than each bin and weighted down with bricks, is a cheap sort of lid. Hinged lids are more classy and expensive. What I dream of is a custom-made 'fertiliser station' (see illus-

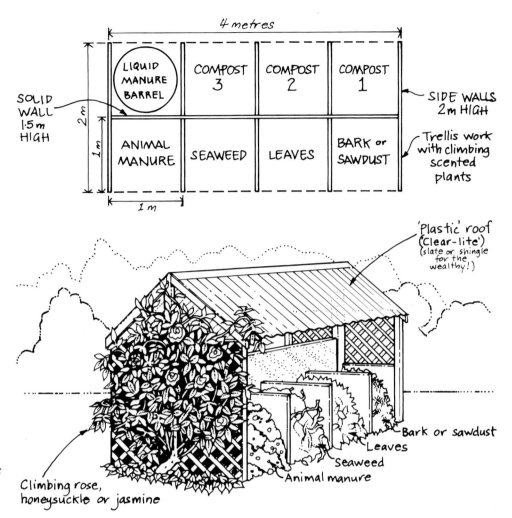

The ultimate in convenience – a custom-made fertiliser station.

tration), with spaces for storing animal manures, leaf mould, liquid manure and wood ash, as well as compost. With roses and honeysuckle scrambling over it, this could be an attractive as well as useful feature of the vegetable garden.

Having got the right sort of bins in the right sort of place, what do you do next?

Start loading Bin One with all the waste organic matter you can find. This includes weeds – but not weeds with ripe seed heads, unless you are sure that your compost will get hot enough to kill them, and not weeds like convolvulus that can grow again from inadequately composted pieces. Other candidates for the compost bin include soft (i.e. non-woody) prunings, kitchen scraps, seaweed, shredded newspaper, vacuum cleaner fluff, un-treated sawdust (in *small* amounts), comfrey and other herb leaves, wool, hair, and so on. A little bit of soil will go in with the weeds, and this is fine. The smaller, softer, more evenly sized the material you put in, the faster and finer your compost will come out. So chop up anything that looks at all tough. (There are shredders designed to do this chopping for you, allowing you to make use of a wider range of organic materials, but they are not cheap.) As your heap builds up, you can add a patent compost activator, or yarrow leaves, or a sprinkling of especially rich soil as an aid to speeding up decomposition. If, like me, you can't be bothered, you will still get accept-able compost eventually.

When your first bin is full, make sure it is damp but not wet, cover it, leave it and start filling Bin Three. *Not* Bin Two. After three or four weeks in summer (longer in winter) you can then turn the compost in Bin One – that is, shovel it out of Bin One into Bin Two. This is a sort of 'sides to middle' process which gives the bits on the sides which are rotting more slowly a chance to get to a hotter spot, which speeds up the composting. But if you are lazy, too busy, or disabled, you can omit this energetic step and just wait a little longer for your compost.

Bin Two is now full, Bin Three almost full, and Bin One ready to be filled again. When Bin Two is ready to be shovelled on to the garden, you can turn the contents of Bin Three into it . . . and so on . . . Get it? An endless cycle of recycling – just like nature, only more work.

How do you use your compost once it is made? Some people dig it into the garden but I think that if you're going to go to this trouble, you may as well use the cheats' method of composting, which is to dig a long, deep trench, fill it with compostables, cover it with soil, and then wait till the waste rots down and the trench is fit to plant on. This is a very good method if you lack space for compost bins and/or enough garden waste to fill them. Good compost from bins, however, is best used as a mulch, spread around the plants or just lightly raked or forked into the soil. If your garden has as many earthworms as a good organic garden should, they will start dragging the compost down to the plants' roots, and between them and the process of decomposition which continues in the mulch you will be wondering where it went so fast.

If you keep feeding your soil with good compost and a variety of other organic manures, you will not need to buy any artificial fertilisers. However, you will probably need to buy some lime to stop the soil in your heavily fertilised vege garden from getting too acid for those crops (asparagus, beet-root, broccoli, cabbage, cucumber, garlic, lettuce, onions, peas, silverbeet, spinach) which prefer neutral or slightly alkaline soil. The lime to use is dolomite, which is a mixture of magnesium and calcium carbonates and thus maintains a balance of calcium and magnesium in the soil. You can buy soil-testing kits to find out if your soil is too acid or alkaline for veges (and for lime-loving or -hating ornamentals). On the pH scale of 0 to 14, neutral is between 6.5 and 7.5; acid below 7.0 and alkali above. Most veges will grow in 5.5–7.0 soils, so you have some leeway, but a near-neutral 6.5–7.0 is most desirable. If you want to get scientific about it, the testing kits are fun, but it is quite possible to get by the way I do – by adding a handful or two of dolomite every other year to beds which are going to have crops which don't like acid soils.

Soil and Plant Care

It is hard to separate caring for your soil from caring for your plants, as the two are so interconnected. What needs to be taken into consideration in maintaining your garden in a happy, healthy condition?

Madonna lilies and double opium poppies grow to perfection in this tidy cottage garden. Mysterious bunches of brushwood may be protection for young plants.
ALEXANDER TURNBULL LIBRARY

1. Cultivation

Do you need to dig? This is not a silly question – today's cunning cottage gardeners take a tip from nature and do as little digging as possible. There are two ways to avoid digging. The thorough way is to design a total 'no dig' garden, consisting of raised beds which are filled with organic matter (straw, paper, compost), planted, and maintained by compost mulching. The contemporary populariser of this sort of garden is Esther Deans who has written several books on the subject.

The compromise way is to dig the ground thoroughly once (this is especially important if the ground has not been gardened before), make any additions or alterations necessary such as adding compost and altering the pH, then to plant it up and maintain it thereafter by mulching (see below). In the flower garden this system will keep things going indefinitely. Digging will be necessary only when old plantings are broken up and shifted and new ones are added.

If in the vegetable garden you have designed a series of small beds, potager style, it is necessary only to fork over the soil, incorporating some compost or animal manure, whenever you clear a bed of one crop and want to prepare it for the next. A lot of New Zealanders dig their gardens all over at least once a year, usually in spring, mainly to deal with the weeds which have grown in the ground left empty over winter. If crop succession is planned correctly and green manuring is practised, it is quite possible to avoid this annual and daunting chore, which puts many people off vegetable gardening or drives them to the use of environmentally insensitive petrol-powered cultivators.

93

2. Mulching and watering

The key to avoiding digging is mulching, or the application of materials to the surface of the soil. English gardening writer Roy Genders expresses the ideal thus:

The cottage garden needs neither hoe nor hose to maintain the plants in healthy condition. Only an occasional mulch of decayed manure and leaf mould such as the plants received during the time when they grew in their native habitat and when the ground was covered with leaves which decayed and provided them with humus.[1]

The connection between mulching and watering is well made and is especially relevant to drier parts of New Zealand. A heavy mulch applied after a thorough watering is a time-honoured way of conserving moisture. A well-mulched flower garden is more likely to survive periods of drought, when all available water is needed to keep vegetables growing, than a garden with bare soil exposed to drying sun and wind.

So what do you mulch with? Compost is ideal for flowers and vegetables, as it feeds the soil as well as keeping in moisture. Straw is a classic mulch, which eventually rots into the ground, and dry grass clippings can be used in the same way. *Untreated* and *well-aged* sawdust can be used also – but if you're not sure how old it is, spread it over an organic manure in a thin layer, as too much will rob the soil of nitrogen. Leaf mould (rotted leaves), pine needles and pine bark (shredded or chunky) are good mulches for plants which like acid soil. Shredded bark is ideal for native plants. Seaweed, preferably chopped up, is a good all-purpose mulch, but keep fresh seaweed away from young plants. The use of comfrey as a mulch has already been mentioned, and the waste of some factories, such as cocoa husks and wool shoddy, can also be used. A common and popular inorganic mulch is black polythene sheeting, which is clean and convenient and raises soil temperature (important for early or slow-growing crops) as well as keeping in moisture. However, most cottage gardeners will prefer the more natural look and soil-feeding properties of organic mulches.

Mulching will not relieve you of the necessity to water the garden altogether, but it will help the ornamental garden to be self-sufficient for longer. Another possibility for reducing water evaporation is to grow plants close together so that their leaves touch and shade the ground. Cottage gardeners do this anyway because they hate the sight of bare earth – a sight seen in nature only in deserts or following catastrophes such as landslides. It is very easy to achieve full coverage in the flower garden and also desirable in the vegetable garden. Vegetables grown in deep, rich soil in small beds, well mulched with organic material, do not need to be spaced as widely apart as the seed packets recommend. Those distances are designed as guides to growers who use artificial fertilisers, cultivate the soil frequently and want to grow large, heavy vegetables. If you are happy with smaller vegetables, and more of them, experiment with closer plantings. How close you can go will of course depend on the vegetable being grown. Spring onions can be tightly packed, but it would be foolish to try to grow beetroots so close together that the roots touch. Space your sowing so as to give the plant room to reach maturity unhindered, plus a little 'breathing space'.

Watering a well-mulched garden requires special care. Sprinkling from on high may lead to the water landing only on the closely packed leaves and quickly evaporating. You may need to supplement overhead waterings or use systems which deliver water at ground level.

3. Crop rotation and companion planting

To get the best out of your vegetable garden it is essential to rotate the crops. This means not replanting vegetables in the same place. There are some exceptions to this rule, such as asparagus, which needs a permanent bed, but most crops benefit from being moved. Why? First, because rotation deprives soil-borne pests and diseases of an opportunity to fasten on to the crop of their choice. Second, it allows the feeding requirements of different crops to be regularly attended to.

I use the five-year rotation system devised by the organic-gardening experts at Lincoln College, as described in Richard Llewellyn Hudson's *Organic Gardening in New Zealand*. By the back door I have taped a chart which looks like this:

Potatoes	Peas	Cabbage	Carrots	Sweet
	Beans	Broccoli	Parsnips	corn
Onions	Tomatoes	Cauliflower		
Garlic	Peppers	Kale	Celery	*or*
Leeks	Cucumber			Green
Shallots	Courgettes		Lettuce	manure
	Pumpkin		Artichoke	
Spinach	Squash		Chicory	*or*
Beets				Fallow

When I clear a bed of one crop I check the chart to see what should go in next and prepare the soil accordingly before planting the next succession. A little knowledge of the way the seasons work in your area is necessary to make this system work most effectively. In the southern parts of New Zealand tomatoes, peppers and aubergines are usually grown under glass, and you must plan ahead to make sure that empty beds are ready and waiting for crops like pumpkins and sweet corn which take longer to grow and ripen. If you slip up you can always double up crops in one bed so long as they belong to the same part of the rotation – for example, leeks with spinach, lettuce with carrots. Although this system is called five-year rotation, I prefer to think of it as a five-point rotation because peas which are in the ground from September to January can be followed by cabbages which occupy the same bed from February to July. The bed can then be well manured in August and be ready for planting lettuce which you'll be eating by Christmas.

Following the rotation will seem a bit tricky for the first year, but eventually you will memorise the sequence. When you've done that, you may be ready to add a further complication which many cottage gardeners swear by – companion planting. Companion planting is based on observations by generations of gardeners that some plants grow well together and some just

Special details can add charm to a garden. These slate labels at Linnaeus' Garden at Uppsala, Sweden, are a unique example.

don't get on. Plants that do well together may be exchanging beneficial substances via their roots and leaves, or one plant may contain a chemical substance which discourages a pest or disease which favours the other plant. Similarly, plants which don't do well together may not like each other's 'chemistry'.

When you think of how many types of vegetables and herbs there are, the possibilities for combinations and separations are legion. There are several books (see Bibliography) which advise on the details of companion planting. Richard Llewellyn Hudson in *Organic Gardening in New Zealand* lists the ones which New Zealand gardeners have found useful. These include garlic and chives under roses to deter aphids (I use garlic chives whose pretty white flower heads team well with my old roses), beans with corn for improved yields of both plants, and marigolds in glasshouses to deter nematodes and white fly. This is obviously an interesting area of study for gardeners with the time and patience to experiment and record their observations. If, like me, you like the idea but are short of time, you can make do with moving your crops on regularly so that they get to grow in different parts of the garden alongside different companions, and with planting lots of herbs in and around your veges. Some herbs, such as tansy and wormwood, smell like they would deter anything, while others, such as hyssop and borage, with their blue flowers, attract beneficial insects like bees. The method is not scientific, but it is satisfying – and definitely sweeter and safer than putting on gloves, overalls and face mask and spraying stinky chemicals.

Pest and Disease Control

Companion planting is only one rather fuzzy method of organic protection against garden pests and diseases. Cottage gardeners begin defending themselves by paying attention to proper soil health and hygiene. Good healthy soil produces good healthy plants, better able to resist the bugs and bertie germs of the garden. This works most of the time, but what do you do when it is not enough?

You practise an organic version of IPM (Integrated Pest Management), that's what. IPM is based on the premise that you can anticipate and outsmart the bad beasties without resorting to chemical overkill. Chemical pest control exercises your wallet, IPM uses your brain. So what do you need to know about common garden pests and diseases to keep them at bay? Here are a few hints, arranged according to the type of problem.

Diseases
• Be meticulous in removing weeds like groundsel and Yorkshire fog which are likely to harbour rusts which will spread to your veges.
• Grow resistant varieties of plants.
• Time your plantings of vulnerable crops so as to avoid weather conditions likely to promote fungal diseases.
• Keep the garden clean – all prunings, weeds, and so on should be composted or otherwise disposed of quickly.
• If buying in plants, make sure they are healthy.

As popular today as they were a century ago, parallel herbaceous borders set this shingled cottage off to perfection.
AUCKLAND INSTITUTE AND MUSEUM

Insect pests

• Encourage beneficial insects which eat the undesirables. Ladybirds and praying mantises are well known, but various beetles, lacewings and other insects are also carnivorous, and it is worth getting to know the insects in your garden better so that you don't destroy the useful ones by mistake.

• Use traps of different kinds. Traps can include saucers of beer for slugs, and folded sacking for slaters and other bugs which like dark hideaways. Brown sugar water solution, or fermented port wine, in jars set in trees, will attract leafroller moths. Sweet yeasty solutions in jars – for example, banana peel, vegemite and water – attract fruit flies which drown in the mixture. Richard Llewellyn Hudson (*Organic Gardening in New Zealand*) and Jackie French (*The Organic Garden Doctor*) have further suggestions.

• Spray them – with water. Hose off soft pests like aphids. If you haven't got time to do this, there are some organic sprays and dusts you can use. Don't forget that most of these sprays are still *poisonous*, and you must mix, apply and store them with care. The reason why they are permitted in organic gardens is that, unlike the synthetic chemicals, they do not leave long-term poisonous residues in the soil. The substances which can be used in the organic garden include pyrethrum, derris, chilli pepper, soft soap, tobacco and rhubarb. Methods for preparation can be found in *Organic Gardening in New Zealand* and other organic gardening books. There are also some organically acceptable commercial preparations available, such as *Bacillus thuringiensis*, a bacterium which attacks moths. Other preparations are based on fatty acids which do not leave dangerous residues.

Other pests

• Slugs and snails can be deterred from attacking your seedlings by putting 'rough stuff' around the plants – that is, something which is going to feel like sandpaper or needles to their soft undersides, such as coarse grit or brushwood. Otherwise hand removal is better than poison pellets, because you might accidentally poison a garden friend with a lethal slug.

• Encourage garden friends. In New Zealand these are hedgehogs, birds and friendly insects. Hedgehogs can be encouraged to stay around with small, occasional feeds of canned pet food (better for them than bread and milk), an appetiser before they move on to your slugs and snails. Some people try to keep birds out of their gardens because they sometimes dig up seeds or peck fruit. As someone who believes that bird song, bird colour and bird flight are among the great joys of a garden, I keep a well-stocked bird table in winter, plant trees which birds like to feed on for the rest of the year, and welcome all comers, especially native birds, which eat insects, berries and nectar, not seeds. Blackbirds flicking your nice neat mulches over the paths can be tiresome – until you remember that they are after slugs and caterpillars. My garden is home or hotel to a dozen species of bird and the most I have ever lost to them is a few plums. Perhaps this is because of my policy of providing them with lots of delicacies they like, such as nectar and berry-bearing trees and shrubs, so that in return they leave my delicacies alone. Isn't it better to have an overstocked garden full of occasionally naughty feathered friends than a chemically sanitised garden and no friends at all?

Successful organic IPM is based on two premises: 'know your enemy' and 'reward your friends'. The more you understand about garden ecology and how to maintain the 'balance of nature', the less likely you are to be caught short by unexpected and uncontrollable pests and diseases. But perhaps more important than the contents of your mind is the state of your mind. If you can feel relaxed about losing a few plants to creatures who are faster and hungrier than you, if you are able to be flexible in figuring out how to outwit them next time, if you don't mind cutting round the odd spot or blemish on fruit, if you can stop to enjoy the flight of the white butterflies before rushing for the derris dust, pest and disease control will shrink to manageable proportions and not be the big bogey it is made out to be by those with a financial interest in pest and disease-control products. Remember, the chemical companies stand to make big profits if they can persuade you to buy into their unhealthy obsession with total chemical control of nature. Who needs it? Not the cottage gardener . . .

Plant Propagation

If you find it fun to interfere with nature, propagating plants offers a lot more rewards than dosing them. Propagating your own plants is the key to the well-stocked cottage garden.

The majority of cottage garden plants are easily propagated from seeds, cutting or division. You will soon learn which are the fastest and easiest to

grow, and for a while your garden may reflect this! If you have never propagated plants before, you will find a book like *The Hamlyn Guide to Plant Propagation*, edited by Suzanne Mitchell and Barbara Haynes, very good value for relatively little money. It uses clear black and white photos to demonstrate how to grow plants from seed, from cuttings, by root division, by layering, by budding and grafting and by dividing bulb offsets.

To start propagating your own plants you will need:

• 1 large bag of seed-raising mix (the commercial kinds all give good results and are less trouble than making your own);

• 2 large bags of sand (clean, coarse river sand, which you can buy from a garden centre, not fine, salty sea sand);

• 2 large bags of peat;

• 1 large bag of compost (the commercial kind won't contain the weed seeds which yours might);

• seed-raising trays, punnets and pots. These can be improvised – blue polystyrene mushroom boxes begged from greengrocers are good, and plastic food containers (butter, margarine, yoghurt, etc.) can be used if drainage holes are punched in the bottom with a large nail. Save all the punnets and pots you buy plants in too.

• plastic bags or pots for transplanting seedlings or for plant cuttings to grow on till big enough for planting out. The three-quarter or one-and-a-half sized plastic bags (PBs) from the garden centre are big enough and inexpensive. The equivalent size in pots is dearer, but less trouble to fill with potting mix and move about. Both bags and pots can be used over and over again if you wash them well between plants to prevent transmission of disease.

• wooden or plastic sticks for labelling trays and pots, and a marker pen or pencil. The little flat wooden sticks used for lollipops or iceblocks are cheapest, but not as clear as plastic labels.

• a watering can with a fine rose;

• a sharp knife for taking cuttings;

- various homemade devices for tamping down seed mixes (e.g., a large, flat block of wood) and pricking out seedlings (e.g., an old pen or pencil, teaspoon or skewer).

A final luxury is a glasshouse or shadehouse with shelves built to hold trays and pots, and a workbench. If you don't have this desirable building you will have to make creative use of what you have already – warm sports in the house such as the hot-water cupboard or a sunny porch or verandah, and sheltered spots, frames or cloches in the garden.

Once you have got the right gear together, you can start following instructions for the particular plant you want to grow. Most seeds will oblige if sprinkled on thoroughly damp and firmly packed seed-raising mix, covered with another layer of mix related to the size of the seed (the larger the seed the deeper the layer) and kept warm, dark and damp until they germinate. However, some seeds respond better if left uncovered, and others like first to be chilled (to simulate natural conditions), soaked or chipped (to crack hard coats). Check before you sow (read the packet or consult a book) to avoid disappointment.

Most seeds can be sown most times of the year, but spring and summer will probably suit you best. Cuttings of herbaceous plants are usually taken in summer or autumn, and if properly tended will put on enough growth in autumn and winter to be planted out the following spring or summer. The thrifty cottage gardener will find out which plants that are easily propagated from cuttings suit her planting schemes; acquire enough cuttings in the summer of one year and have a stock of new plants ready to plant out the following spring.

Once you have checked on the correct time of year to take cuttings of your favoured plants, slice off a piece 10–12 cm long with a sharp knife. Cut just below a node (where leaves join the stem) and put your cutting straight into a jar of water so that it doesn't dry out. (Some plants can be left there, as they will root in water alone.) Trim your cutting of most of its leaves. The larger the leaf, the fewer you should leave on, and very large leaves should be cut in half. Dip the base of the cutting into the appropriate proprietary hormone rooting powder – softwood for soft green cuttings and hardwood for woody ones.

If you use these commercial powders, you must replace them every two to three years to maintain freshness, even though you are unlikely to have run out of powder in that time. Organic purists may like to substitute these with willow water (water in which willow leaves have been soaked), or you can put the cutting straight into the soil without any hormone dressing at all. If your soil mixture is right (three parts very coarse sand, two parts peat and one part good soil or compost suits most plants) and you keep it damp, warm and lightly shaded, you still have a good chance of success. (If you can't visualise 'parts' of sand, peat and compost, try thinking of it as three *buckets* of sand, two of peat and one of compost, all well mixed together.)

How do you find out when to propagate what, and the propagating preferences of each species? The likes and dislikes of hundreds of plants is a daunting subject, and if you don't have access to a friendly horticulturist or a wise old gardener (which you can easily have if you join the local horticultural

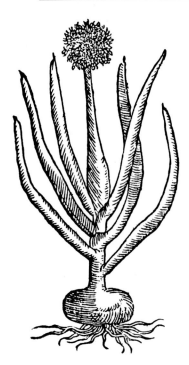

society or gardening club), your best bet is a subscription to the *New Zealand Gardener* and regular trips to the library to consult books by expert gardeners like Christopher Lloyd (see Bibliography) who are happy to share their personal experience of propagating under amateur rather than commercial conditions. If you intend doing a lot of propagating it is worth keeping an indexed notebook in which you record the preferences of the plants you are working with. For the trickier kinds of propagation such as grafting, you would be advised to join the local horticultural society, so that you can attend demonstrations at which experts share their skills, and make friends with people whom you can ask for advice.

How Much to Grow for Self-sufficiency

Can you really opt out of the market economy on a quart r acre, and live well? How much land do you need to set aside for growing produce?

My calculation, for two adults who are vegetarians and who grow twenty-five different varieties of vegetable in an intensive potager style, is that you will need to devote sixty to sixty-five square metres to vegetable production. How much you should grow of each type of vegetable will depend on your personal preferences and what part of New Zealand you live in, but this amount of land will allow you to be self-sufficient in a reasonable range of vegetables. How much space you need to devote to soft fruits will again depend on your preferences. But three blackcurrant bushes, two redcurrant bushes, two gooseberry bushes, forty to fifty strawberry plants, twenty to thirty well-grown raspberry (or blackberry, loganberry, boysenberry) canes, and three clumps of rhubarb will produce plenty for both fresh fruit and preserves for two adults.

For tree fruit you will want to plant a succession of apple trees from early dessert apples through to late cookers. Half a dozen trees should cover the gamut. Three pear trees could also cover the early, middle and late sequence. Plant two trees each of stone fruit (apricot, nectarine, peach, cherry, plum) if you live in a cooler district; substitute tamarillo, loquat, avocado, citrus, persimmon and other subtropicals in warmer areas. Don't forget the vines – grape, passionfruit, kiwifruit – which can grow over pergolas and fences as well as purpose-built structures. Some other fruit trees – avocado, walnut, lemon, orange and persimmon – make handsome specimen trees, while dwarf varieties can grace terraces and other formal parts of the garden. Then there are fruits which can be grown as hedges – feijoas, cranberry and hazelnut. Finally there are the 'wild' fruits – elderberry, rosehip, rowanberry, crab apple and japonica apple – which can be grown as ornamental parts of the garden.

A fruitful garden need not look like a commercial orchard. Even if trees are grown in rows, naturalised bulbs, self-seeding annuals (poppies, granny's bonnets, cornflowers, and so on) and green ground covers can be grown underneath them. This may reduce the yield a little, but not too much if you keep the trees heavily mulched with compost out to the 'drip line' (the edge of the branches). Don't let mulches touch the bark as they may harbour pests or encourage rot. Experiments are currently being conducted into underplanting fruit trees with herbs which will deter insect pests. An under-

ABOVE:

Common, versatile and under-appreciated – manuka is ideal for cottage garden seats, fences or archways and deserves a better fate than the woodburner.

RIGHT:

Massed planting or planting in drifts creates a more pleasing and natural effect than skimping on plant material – here, Primula beesiana.

planted orchard provides a pleasant place for children to play and for you to relax with a book on a hot summer's day. After all, the point of self-sufficiency is to reduce your cares, not multiply them.

To be self-sufficient in herbs requires less space but some careful fore-thought about how often you use your favourites and what you use them for. Here are some flexible rules for the most popular herbs.

Parsley is used almost every day, so three or even four large plants is not too many. It is a biennial with an annoying habit of going to seed just when you need it most, so remember to plant new plants at regular intervals. Curled parsley is most commonly grown, but the flat-leaf parsley is just as tasty in cooked dishes and can be used for decorative effects – for example, as an alternative to coriander in decorating Asian dishes.

Chives' mauvy-pink flowers are so attractive and quick growing that it is necessary to have several plants to enjoy both flowers and leaves.

Bulbs are ideal for naturalising. They establish easily and, like these fritillaries, can create a spectacular spring show.

Chervil and basil are small, tender herbs, and several plants are needed to keep up a good supply for the kitchen, especially if (in the case of basil) you are fond of Mediterranean cooking. Basil is difficult to grow outdoors in cool and/or windy places: grow it in large pots in the glasshouse or indoors if your garden is at all exposed.

Unless you make inordinate amounts of stuffing, one sage and one thyme plant will suffice for your need of these fresh herbs. Only if you wish to dry them for winter will another one or two plants be necessary. Do consider the flavoured thymes (especially lemon and caraway) and pineapple sage as pleasant alternatives to the common varieties. Remember also that common sage and pineapple sage have beautiful flowers, the bluish-mauve of the former being very attractive to bees. Sage also makes a very virtuous herb tea: if you take to it you will need several bushes.

Mint can usually take care of itself, especially the rust-free varieties which are now available. Spearmint is the kind commonly grown for mint sauce and for Middle Eastern cookery, although apple mint will do. Peppermint is better saved for teas – one sprig in a cup, infuse and remove like a teabag. Eau de cologne mint is worth growing in quantity for 'green baths' which aren't nearly as fiddly and time-consuming to prepare as you'd expect. The most effective way I know of making a herb bath is to fill a cooking pot with roughly chopped eau de cologne mint and lemon balm, add water to cover, put on the lid, bring to the boil, turn off the heat and let stand to cool. Strain the green liquid into a hot bath for a refreshing soak.

One plant each of the less common culinary herbs – tarragon, lemon balm, borage, comfrey, salad burnet, fennel, lovage, dill, coriander and sweet cicely – will be enough for households with traditional Anglo-Saxon tastes. Anyone who prefers European or Asian cooking will want more of herbs like tarragon, dill and coriander.

If you intend drying your herbs for winter use as flavourings or teas, you will need to grow more. Three or four chamomile plants will provide

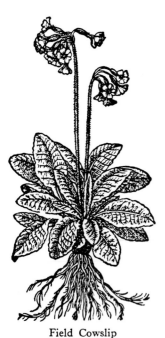

Field Cowslip

enough dried flowers for tea in households which use it like Peter Rabbit's mother – to alleviate headaches, strain and digestive upsets.

Medicine, dye and scent are more specialised uses for herbs: you will have to consult the recipes of any herbal products you intend to make regularly and try to estimate how many plants you will need to be self-sufficient. The average suburban garden gets away with barely a square metre of herbs, but I think a true cottage garden should have at least ten square metres devoted to them, even though some of the plantings, such as lavender and old roses for pot-pourri, culinary fennel in a border and borage to attract bees, may double as ornamental plantings.

Cross-cultural Considerations: Advice for Northern Gardeners

Most of the traditional cottage garden flowering plants are native to north European countries where winters are colder and harsher, summers are cooler and shorter, and rain is frequent and gentle. Plants which evolved under these conditions adapted to them. They learned to grow fast in summer, take a rest in winter, and enjoy small 'drinks' often. They managed to outwit some pests and diseases by setting seed or disappearing underground before they were eaten alive.

When these plants were brought to New Zealand, and especially to the northern parts, they had to make adjustments or pine and perish. Plants which have spent millions of years evolving to a perfectly adapted state can't make a total adjustment (unaided) in a mere century or so – which is why a lot of English cottage garden plants are less than totally happy in New Zealand conditions. Our winters are much milder, so the plants don't get their well-deserved rest and chance to escape from predators and parasites. The rain either comes in buckets, or it doesn't come at all. The gorgeous imported plants which really flourish without assistance in New Zealand are those from southern Africa, not northern Europe.

Gardeners in the southern parts of New Zealand can therefore grow a wider range of traditional cottage plants than those in the north. If you are one of the majority of New Zealanders who live north of Taupo, you are going to need the following information on how to avoid failure in your attempts to grow a flowery cottage garden.

Basically, your best strategy is simply to forget about the plants which need cold winters and/or gentle, damp summers to grow well (and avoid pests and diseases), and to concentrate on some of the equally attractive newer alternatives which will look just as pretty in a cottage garden-style border. After consulting experienced growers in Auckland and the Bay of Plenty, I compiled the following list of 'northern no-hopers':

• *Pulsatilla, Aconitum, Hepatica, Fritillaria, Paeonia* (paeony), *Althaea* (hollyhock), *Convallaria, Polygonum* (Solomon's seal), *Astrantia, Corydalis, Lavandula* (*L. angustifolia* or 'English' lavender), *Malva* (mallow), *Sidalcea, Verbascum, Lupinus* (Russell lupin), *Pulmonaria, Tulipa* (tulips), *Cardiocrinum, Scilla, Iris* (bearded iris).

Marginal, but possible in the right (that is, cool, shady) spot are:

- *Helleborus* (hellebores), *Leucojum* (snowflakes), *Salvia officinalis* (sage), *Stachys officinalis* (betony), *Chamaemelum* (chamomile), *Viola odorata* (violet), *Hyssopus* (hyssop) and *Anethum graveolens* (dill).

In fact, most herbs like a cooler climate and dislike heavy rain.

If you live in northern parts, you are bound to note with triumph that at least one of these 'northern no-hopers' is doing very well in your garden. But perhaps the general rule will also explain why some traditional treasures have turned up their toes for you.

Before listing the cottagey plants that will thrive in warm, wet conditions, I have a few more tips to pass on.

Time it

Most of New Zealand does not experience winter as it is known in Britain and northern Europe. Our milder winters and springs mean that European flowering plants start flowering earlier, especially in northern parts of New Zealand. Gardeners in northern New Zealand should not try to imitate English gardeners and time their main displays of flowers for the second month of summer. By late spring and early summer they will find European perennials are reaching their peak and by New Year they will be flopping about. What can be done about this?

One strategy is to 'go with the flow'. Aim to have the garden at its picturesque best for Christmas, then cut everything back hard and go away for a holiday in January. By February, if weather conditions are normal, you should get a reprise. You can be sure this will happen if you also plant flowers which are at their best in late summer anyway. These include many members of the colourful and varied Compositae family such as *Rudbeckia*, *Heliopsis*, *Coreopsis* and *Brachycome*, and the South African bulbs such as *Amaryllis*, *Crocosmia*, *Kniphofia*, *Agapanthus* and *Schizostylis*. You can also hold back plantings of some flowers like *Verbascum* and *Malva*, and aim to have them out in February, not December, when they will do better. If you get a new perennial and you are not sure when it will peak, put it somewhere inconspicuous for the first season until you gauge its mettle. Don't shift it to pride of place unless you are sure it can handle it.

Cool it

In northern New Zealand it is necessary to rethink the definition of a tender cottage garden plant. Here European plants need not fear the frost and snow, but sun. Some of the 'marginals' and 'no-hopers' may be grown if the right spot is found for them – for example, in south-facing, shady borders. *Convallaria* (lily-of-the-valley), *Polygonum* (Solomon's seal), *Scilla* (bluebells), *Leucojum* (snowflakes) and *Helleborus* (hellebores) will do better like this. But for flowers like tulips and paeonies, which must have a good freeze in winter, it will never be cold enough, and northern growers should look at equally bright and beautiful substitutes from among the range of South African bulbs and corms.

'The Garden at East Tamaki', c. 1880. The romantic European idea of flower gardening was transported to Auckland with the first European settlers.

AUCKLAND CITY ART GALLERY

Drain it

Cottage garden flowers hate wet feet. If you can't provide a well-drained soil, consider specialising in bog and water plants. If, like so many Aucklanders, you are gardening on heavy clay which you can't keep dry in winter, lift your fussy perennials in autumn and replant in spring.

Cut it

Paradoxically, you can improve your perennials in warm climates by cutting them back hard. Put them in as *young* plants: don't let them get cramped in their containers or they may suffer a permanent check. Pinch their tops back hard when they are in their first flush of growth to encourage them to bush out rather than grow long and lanky. Then cut them back hard after their first flowering and you should get another one.

Don't bother with it

Some cottage garden plants will grow in northern New Zealand, but they won't produce the highly coloured foliage for which they are famous in their native land. Coloured plantains are one example of this – rosy-purple in Southland and very lacklustre in Auckland. Trees grown for autumn foliage must also be chosen with care – poplars which flame into golden yellow in Central Otago go rusty-brown and flop in Auckland, for example. Most plants need cold to colour up, so keep your eyes open in autumn for what looks best in your area rather than following advice in foreign garden books.

Autumn foliage can be selected for dramatic effect and toning with buildings like this American weatherboard cottage.
OLD SALEM

Recover it

The big problem with attempting a natural or wild style of garden in northern New Zealand is that weeds which are restrained in Europe are rampant here and quickly smother your little cottage treasures. One way to deal with this is to rethink your attitude towards weeds. Some of the wilder weeds of Auckland, such as *Zantedeschia* (arum lilies), *Crocosmia* (montbretia) and *Hedychium* (wild ginger) would be the envy of many a European gardener. And why should we pine for drifts of snowdrops and bluebells when *Arthropodium* (rengarenga lilies) and *Agapanthus* will give us the same colour effects with more dramatic foliage? (Agapanthus is regarded as common in New Zealand, but what could be more common than bluebells in England?) We should be looking for local combinations of the commonplace which are as inspired as those of the great Australian designer, Edna Walling. Her avenue of gum trees underplanted with watsonias, two very ordinary and even 'weedy' southern hemisphere plants, is a lesson in deriving beauty from simplicity.

But if you still want a derivative English effect in the sub-subtropics then you will have to resort to technology. Hopefully not chemical technology – I am always gratified (in a depressed sort of way) at seeing how weeds can totally smother an area which was sprayed at great expense with the best

HYACINTHS IN POT.

weedkiller only three months previously. The nicer inorganic alternative is 'Weed Mat', a very fine mesh which will suppress weeds while letting the soil breathe. Covered with bark and of course the leaves of your plants, it will look almost as natural as natural and save a lot of weeding.

Avoid it

Don't make a rod for your back by favouring plants which are prone to pests and diseases in your area. Hollyhocks and snapdragons are cottage classics which are sadly susceptible in hot, humid climates, so until resistant varieties are developed they are not worth persisting with. Unless you *like* spraying roses for black spot, mildew and other diseases, you will put resistance up there with scent and colour on the top of your rose checklist.

Drat it!

Some things which make European perennials a better bet in southern rather than northern New Zealand you just can't do a thing about. Like the length of summer daylight in your area. Unless you have some influence with Maui and can get him to come back and hold the sun over your house, your perennials will just have to make do with what they get naturally – which in southern New Zealand is up to three hours more daylight in summer than northern New Zealand. It is light rather than heat which pulls European perennials upwards, so the tallest delphiniums in New Zealand will always grow in Southland, not Northland. Northlanders harvesting bananas (which respond to heat, not light) probably won't be too put out at the thought, and that's the essence of cottage gardening. Find out what does best in your area, and do it well.

So here are some suggestions for five-star perennials or self-sowing annuals for cottage gardens in northern New Zealand:

Platycodon, Dicentra, Salvia (especially *S. uliginosa*), *Geranium, Erigeron, Anemone japonica, Gaura lindheimeri, Aquilegia, Lychnis, Gaillardia, Rudbeckia, Coreopsis, Omphalodes, Potentilla, Eupatorium, Nicotiana, Geum, Viola, Tweedia, Lythrum, Stokesia, Aster, Armeria, Silene, Teucrium, Veronica, Papaver orientale, Filipendula, Heliotrope, Primula* (especially the tall ones, *P. dentata, P. capitata, P. viallia*), *Polemonium, Inula, Thalictrum, Lobelia cardinalis, Dierama, Liatris, Scabiosa, Centranthus, Scuttelaria, Macleaya cordata.*

Further advice on what does well in Auckland conditions can be obtained from the Auckland Regional Botanic Gardens at Manurewa, which has pamphlets on plants best suited to Auckland as well as beds and beds full of the best varieties. If you start with the plants listed above, plus the sun-loving bulbs, you'll get a cottagey effect without too much effort fairly quickly. With this success under your belt you are in a much better psychological and practical position to go on to try some of the choice and more finicky traditional cottage garden flowers. But perhaps you will decide that you have created such a distinctively beautiful *New Zealand* cottage garden, by clever combinations of the plants that do well here, that it would be foolish to strive for a half-pie imitation of an English chocolate-box picture.

Chapter 8

COTTAGE
CONNECTIONS

Creating the average New Zealand front garden is not difficult. In *1,000 Years of Gardening in New Zealand*, Helen Leach describes a distinct and increasingly common variant in New Zealand gardening, which she names the 'nurserymen's specials' garden. This sort of garden 'generally features coloured flaxes, purple akeake, silver dollar gum, agonis, red photinias, forsythia, dwarf conifers, boronias, ceanothus and kaka beak, in curious combinations'.[1] This is precisely the effect which cottage gardeners are striving to *avoid*, but it is easy to see why gardeners on limited budgets with an underdeveloped sense of garden style end up with it. It is definitely the path of least resistance. However, with just a little more effort your garden could look so much better.

This chapter focuses on where to find the plants your garden centre doesn't stock, how to learn more about them, where to find gardens which provide ideas and inspiration, how to make contact with cottage gardeners, and other aspects of turning your cottage dreams into practical realities.

In Chapter 5 we looked at how to budget for a cottage garden. Now it is time to find out where to go when your local garden centre suggests that you settle for a magenta pelargonium and a two-tone petunia instead of *Geranium endressi* 'Wargrave's Pink' and *Aquilegia* 'Munstead White'.

There are a number of small nurseries in New Zealand which specialise in perennials, herbs and choice old-fashioned flowers. If you are lucky there will be one near you; if not, you can make use of the mail-order service offered by several excellent suppliers. The annotated listing of cottage plant and seed sellers given in this chapter was up to date at the time of going to press, but please remember that small businesses come and go, and it will pay you to check that any nursery listed here is still in business before you plan a visit or send a cheque. The best way to stay abreast with who is selling what, where, is to check the ads in the *New Zealand Gardener*. Gardens open for visiting and garden tours are also advertised in this monthly magazine, and while most of these are not cottage gardens, most are worth visiting for their trees and flowers seldom seen in suburban gardens and public plantings.

Iris douglasiana

When visiting private gardens and nursery gardens, please remember that plant growers are very like plants – they respond best to considerate attention. It may seem a little basic to have to remind people of simple good manners, but I was surprised to learn how many growers have had visitors who arrive at inconvenient hours without prior notice, ignore 'Closed' signs, steal slips from display gardens, claim to be already growing everything in the nursery, sneer at the stock, expect specialist nurseries to be able to sell them a bottle of weedkiller and a punnet of cabbage seedlings, park their cars in inappropriate places, let their toddler(s) and/or dog(s) rampage through the flower beds, and generally behave in ways conducive to being given a free sample of deadly nightshade and encouraged to eat the delicious berries.

So let me offer a few tips on how to get on the grower's 'favoured customer' list instead.

• Check on the opening hours before you visit. If you want to make a special visit, phone for an appointment.
• Don't pinch cuttings or flowers; leave uncontrollable children and dogs at home; stick to the established paths; park your car in the designated parking space.
• Find out what the nursery/garden specialises in before you visit, and don't go unless you have a genuine interest in what is being grown.
• If you are a beginner, let the grower know what type of soil and climate you are gardening with and what style of garden you are trying to achieve, and then take his or her suggestions seriously. More advanced gardeners should swap cultivation and/or propagation notes and maybe cuttings or seeds.
• Pay admission charges to private gardens graciously. No one is forcing you to visit, and maintaining a private garden to visiting standard takes a lot of time and money. If no admission is charged, but plants and/or other garden products are for sale, do buy something. Plants make wonderful gifts.

Intelligent interest and a willingness to learn and to share are endearing characteristics which will stand you in good stead with everyone, gardeners and growers included. So add them to your list of things to be cultivated by the cottage gardener.

Mail-order nurseries offer an invaluable service for those who can't travel, and some of them now produce detailed, illustrated catalogues which are well worth keeping as reference material. Some tips for successful plant buying by catalogue:
• Get your order in *early*;
• list *substitutes* for your first choice or pay by *limited cheque*; and
• *keep ordering* (at least one 15–20 plant order per year) if you want to keep getting the nursery's catalogue.
Postage or freight charges are of course added on to the cost of the plants themselves, and these rise according to how far away from the nursery you live. It is worth checking whether a nursery in your province or island has what you want before sending 800 kilometres for the same thing. Getting plants which suit your climate is also important, although after visiting mail-

order nurseries in the North Island I can advise that cottage plant growers deliberately put their mail-order plants in cold spots outdoors to ensure that they are hardy anywhere in New Zealand.

Cottage Creativity

The first cottage gardeners were illiterate, but today's cottage gardeners often derive considerable pleasure from reading about their favourite pastime. Pleasure – and profit. If we didn't learn our gardening at mother's knee then a book or magazine full of motherly advice is the next best thing, and saves us from many sad mistakes (or at least provides explanations for our failures). Reference books which New Zealand cottage gardeners will find especially useful or inspiring are listed in the Bibliography, and I have already mentioned the *New Zealand Gardener*, which appears monthly. A quarterly periodical which I find invaluable for organic gardening news and views is *Soil and Health*. It is also a great source of ideas on further uses for your cottage garden produce.

Gardening clubs and societies exist throughout New Zealand, and if you are a 'joiner' these are obvious places to make gardening friends and swap plants. Canny plant collectors frequent plant stalls at school and church fairs – this can also be a good way of finding out who is growing what in your neighbourhood. Invitations to visit gardens should be accepted with alacrity, and garden tours can be a relatively painless way of fundraising for a good cause. Keep your eye open for advertisements for open days, workshops, WEA classes and other opportunities to learn cottage crafts such as dried flower arrangement, making herbal medicines and cosmetics, papermaking, pot-pourri and scent production. If you like reading about gardening and want a good range of books to choose from, write to Touchwood Books, Box 610, Hastings, for their extensive mail-order catalogue of new and second-hand books on plants and gardening.

Your cottage garden can be both a haven and a window on the world, a retreat from activity and a spur to action. It's over to you. Happy gardening!

Nurseries and Gardens

Note: Admission charges to gardens and costs of catalogues are not given as these are subject to change. Unless otherwise stated, all catalogues are charged for.

Southland

The Flower Company,
Redan,
No. 2 R.D.,
Wyndham. Tel: (03) 206 4025
Hours: Sept–May, Sat & Sun 1 pm–5 pm, or by appointment with Johanna Stewart.

Take the road to the Catlins from Wyndham and you'll come to a lovely cottage with an acre of garden and a picnic lawn. Cottage plants and dried flowers for sale.

Marshwood Gardens,
Leonard Road,
West Plains, 4 R.D.,
Invercargill. Tel: (021) 57672
Hours: Spring–Autumn, Wed–Sat 10 am–5 pm; Sun–Tues 1 pm–5 pm. Winter, Sat 12 noon–5 pm only.

An extensive garden with an emphasis on herbs and old-fashioned flowers. A large collection of salvias, and a white garden. Admission charge refundable on purchase of plants. Plants for sale: salvias (list available), delphiniums and lavandulas.

'Floresta' Fragrant Garden,
86 Chelmsford Street,
Invercargill. Tel: (021) 77164
Hours: Sept–March, Mon–Sat 10 am–4 pm.

Half-acre paradise packed with fragrant plants – an inspiration for urban gardeners. Lots of herbs, grown by an expert. No admission charge.

Maple Glen,
Glenham,
Wyndham.
Hours: Sat, dawn to dusk.

Spectacular garden with choice plants on display and for sale. At its peak in spring. No admission charge.

Otago

Larnach Gardens,
Larnach Castle,
Otago Peninsula. Tel: (024) 4761302
Hours: Daily, 9 am–5 pm.

Entry to the nursery is free (tell the gatekeeper you have come to buy plants). Follow the peacocks and Peking ducks to a collection of unusual perennials and native plants.

Mrs A. R. Mitchell,
Clover Hill Plants,
Wairuna, R.D.,
Clinton. Tel: (03) 4157687
Hours: Sat, all day.

Five km south of Clinton and 2 km off State Highway 1 – not yet signposted. Small garden which supplies wholesale perennials to garden centres throughout New Zealand. Mail-order catalogue. Large groups welcome, but prior notice is essential. No admission charge.

Heather and John Metherell,
Southwell Plants,
Hillend, R.D. 2,
Balclutha. Tel: (03) 4182465
Hours: Wed–Sat, all day. Other days by appointment.

A 10-km detour from State Highway 1 to an attractive landscaped country garden and well-stocked nursery of cottage, woodland, alpine and rockery plants. Mail-order catalogue spring and autumn.

Doug and Judy Anderson,
'Garvan',
Lovells Flat,
Milton. Tel: (03) 4174721
Hours: Tues–Sun, 10 am–5 pm.

A beautiful historic home and large 'old world' cottage garden of several acres. Plants for sale. Devonshire teas and lunches at the homestead.

Tregaron Gardens,
Lovells Flat,
State Highway 1,
Milton. Tel: (03) 4178071
Hours: Open daily.

A garden to visit for inspiration and to choose from a range of perennials, alpine and rockery plants for sale.

Millbrook Nursery,
Malaghans Road,
Arrowtown. Tel: (03) 4421491
Hours: Sept–May, Mon–Fri 10 am–5 pm; open Sunday by appointment only.

Old-fashioned roses, herbs and cottage garden plants for sale. Rose list available.

Mrs P. Cook,
Arrow Bulb Farm,
Hunter Road,
No. 1 R.D.,
Queenstown. Tel: (03) 4421525
Hours: Mon–Sat, 9 am–5 pm; Sunday by appointment only.

Large variety of hardy bulbs for sale, as well as a specialty collection of old-fashioned daffodils. Bulb list available.

Lye Bow Alpine Gardens,
Butchers Dam,
R.D. 4,
Alexandra. Tel: (03) 4492124
Hours: Daily, 8 am–6 pm.

On the main road east of Alexandra. Herbs and cottagey flowers as well as choice alpines in a lovely setting.

Bloomin' Plant Nursery,
Goodwin Road, 1 R.D.,
Palmerston. Tel: (03) 4651252
Hours: Mon, Thurs, Fri, 9 am–12 noon, 1.30 pm– 6 pm; Sat–Sun, 9 am–6 pm; other times by arrangement.

Four km east of Palmerston. Proprietor Gill Walker specialises in choice alpines and perennials. Phone for an appointment. A mail-order list is available for a small fee, refundable on first order.

Canterbury

Cottage Plants Limited,
Freepost 356,
Box 18684,
Christchurch 7. Tel: (03) 888748 evenings only

Mail order only. Wide range of plants and prompt, friendly service.

Gethsemene Gardens,
33 Revelation Drive,
Sumner,
Christchurch. Tel: (03) 26 5848
Hours: Mon–Sat, 9 am–5 pm.
A great selection of cottage perennials and a wonderful theme display in a hilltop nursery.

'Weston',
83 Cox Street,
Geraldine. Tel: (03) 693 9092
Hours: March–Nov, Wed–Sat.
A cottage garden which specialises in raising primulas, dianthus, rock and alpine plants, small bulbs and perennials, and with many other plants for sale. Telephone the owner, Margaret Galbraith, for details. Groups welcome by prior arrangement.

Rainbow's End Herb Garden,
Downs Road,
R.D. 21,
Geraldine. Tel: (03) 693 8066
Hours: Oct–March, Wed–Sat, 10 am–6 pm.
Lots of old-fashioned flowers for sale as well as herbs growing to perfection in a classic, formally designed herb garden.

Newlands Rock Gardens,
Orton, R.D. 26,
Temuka. Tel: (03) 615 9828
Rambling rock gardens of different styles. An extensive collection of small-growing plants for sale. Telephone the owner, Bev Davidson, for further details.

Nelson/Marlborough

Thymebank Gardens,
66 Alma Street,
Renwick,
Marlborough. Tel: (057) 28 061
Hours: Open most days.
Great variety of herbs and cottage perennials for sale. Specialises in thymes, salvias, lavenders and geraniums. Catalogue available. Domestic and terracotta pottery.

Oaktree Cottage,
Dashwood,
Marlborough.
Just off State Highway 1 near the Awatere River, well signposted. This restored cob cottage features a traditional garden and cottage flower crafts.

Wellington/Horowhenua/Wairarapa

Pukehou Nursery and Gardens,
State Highway 1,
Manakau. Tel: (069) 26 869
Hours: Aug–Feb, daily; March–July, Mon–Sat.

Very large collection of rockery and perennial plants, with emphasis on cottage classics, annuals and old-world roses. Two acres of landscaped gardens open to public, admission free.

Clareville Nursery,
State Highway 2,
Carterton. Tel: (0593) 8604
Hours: Daily, 9 am–5 pm.
One km north of Carterton. An attractive and educative display garden behind the nursery. A wide range of perennials available. Admission free.

Bennetts Hill Nursery and Garden,
Castlepoint Road,
Nr Masterton. Tel: (059) 81 948
Hours: Wed–Sat, 10 am–4 pm.
Eight km from Masterton. Large country garden around an historic homestead. Over 100 varieties of perennials and a selection of old roses for sale. Admission charge refundable on purchase of plants.

Abbotsford Gardens,
Abbotsford, R.D. 9,
Nr Masterton. Tel: (059) 82 829
Hours: By arrangement.
Twelve km from Masterton on Castlepoint Road. Garden and nursery specialising in foliage and textural accents. Cottage and perennial favourites as well as rare and unusual plants for sale. Admission charge refundable on purchase of plants.

Oakbourne Nursery and Garden,
Annedale Road,
Tinui, via Masterton. Tel: (059) 26 641
Hours: By arrangement.
Large country garden with newly developed picnic area. Changing range of perennials and cottage plants for sale. Admission charge refundable on purchase of plants.

Manawatu/Wanganui/Rangitikei

Westoe Woodland Garden and Nursery,
R.D. 1,
Marton. Tel: (0652) 6350
Hours: Fri & Sat, 10 am–4 pm; other days by arrangement.
Eight km north of Bulls, on the road to Feilding off State Highway 1. Wonderful trees and woodland underplantings. Plants for sale; mail-order and bulb catalogue has some rarities. Admission charge.

The Ridges,
State Highway 1, R.D. 1,
Marton. Tel: (0652) 8279
Hours: Aug–May, Wed–Mon, 10 am–4.30 pm.
Twelve km south of Hunterville. A large country garden with interesting planting. Plants and garden ornaments for sale; mail-order catalogue available. Admission charge; teas and lunches by prior arrangement.

Rathmoy Garden,
Rangatira Road, R.D. 6,
Hunterville. Tel: (0652) 28334
Hours: Oct–mid Dec, 10 am–4.30 pm; other times by
arrangement.

Four km east of Hunterville. A large rural garden with lakes,
waterfowl and farm animals, with plants for sale. Large groups
welcome by prior arrangement. Admission charge; teas and
lunches by arrangement.

Titoki Point,
R.D. 1,
Taihape. Tel: (0658) 80085
Hours: Oct–May, Wed–Sun, 10 am–4 pm.

Signposted from State Highway 1 north of Taihape. Famous
garden with unique collection of plants. Unusual plants for sale.
Admission charge; teas, lunches and campervan sites by prior
arrangement. Groups also by prior arrangement.

Taranaki

Princess Garden Perennials,
Princess Gardens,
Te Roti, R.D. 13,
Hawera. Tel: (062) 28478
Hours: Mon–Fri, 8.30 am–4.30 pm.

Ten km north of Hawera on State Highway. Over 200 varieties
of perennials ranging from the familiar to rare treasures. Mail-
order catalogue available.

Mara Nurseries,
7 High Road,
Hawera. Tel: (062) 87565; 87320 after hours
Hours: Mon–Sat, 9 am–4.30 pm; Sun, 1 pm–4.30 pm.

Cottage and herbaceous border plants for sale. Large display
beds. Mail-order catalogue available.

Hawke's Bay

Peak Perennials,
23 Toop Street/Box 337,
Havelock North. Tel: (070) 776051
Hours: May–Aug, Tues–Sun 10 am–2.30 pm;
Sept–April, Tues–Sun all hours.

Garden and nursery growing over 250 varieties of perennials
and specialising in rarer species and latest releases. The nursery
offers a full mail-order service; send s.a.e. for catalogue.

Millstream Gardens,
Pukehou,
Private Bag,
Hastings. Tel: (06) 8781511
Hours: Variable. Please telephone before visiting.

On State Highway 2, 25 km south of Hastings. A nursery with a
wide range of herbal and fragrant plants and cottage garden
perennials. Mail-order service available throughout year; send
large s.a.e. for catalogue.

Waikato/Bay of Plenty

Karamea Wines and Herbs,
R.D. 10,
Frankton. Tel: (071) 292805
Hours: Tues–Sun, 10 am–6 pm. Closed July.

On Tuhikaramea Road, 4.5 km past Templeview on the way to
Pirongia. Scented geraniums, herbs and old roses are specialties.
There is a herb garden and wine-tasting at the winery. Mail-
order catalogue available.

Bay Bloom Nurseries,
Cambridge Road/P.O. Box 502,
Tauranga. Tel and Fax: (075) 789902
Hours: Wed–Sun, 9 am–5 pm; bus tours and garden
groups any day by appointment.

Two km from corner of Cambridge Road and Tauranga–Waihi
highway. Three acres of display gardens, and a full range of
perennials, old-fashioned roses and bearded and Siberian irises
available. New Zealand's largest mail-order specialists; two full-
colour catalogues a year.

Parva Plants,
Box 2503,
Tauranga. Tel: (075) 24902

Mail-order only. Full-colour catalogue and extensive selection of
choice plants. New goodies always arriving. Cottage specialties:
primroses, old roses and perennials.

Windrest Cottage,
15 Moehau Street,
Te Puke. Tel: (075) 739418
Hours: Oct–March, Sat 1 pm–4 pm, Sun 10 am–4 pm.
Labour Weekend 10 am–4 pm. Other times by
arrangement.

Old-fashioned flowers to view and for sale in this large cottage
garden. Admission charge; Devonshire teas for sale.

Auckland/Northland

'Herbs and Flowers',
Hepburn Creek Road/Box 172,
Warkworth. Tel: (09) 425080
Hours: By arrangement.

Catalogue illustrated with grower's own drawings.

The Old Vicarage Nursery,
73 Trig Road/Box 81026,
Whenuapai. Tel: (09) 4166593
Hours: Sat, Sun & public holidays, 9 am–5 pm for gate
sales.

Mail-order perennials and old roses.

Cottage Gardens Limited,
Stage Highway 1,
Dairy Flat,
Auckland. Tel: (09) 4159372

Hours: Mon–Fri, 9 am–5 pm.

Landscape contractors and wholesale nursery which grows a wide range of trees, shrubs and perennials.

Mulberry Lodge,
149 Popes Road,
Manurewa. Tel: (09) 266 6429
Hours: Nov, Tues–Sat 10 am–4 pm.

Five minutes from the Botanic Gardens. A rambling three-acre garden. Admission charge; no children under five.

Joy Plants,
Runciman Road,
Pukekohe. Tel: (085) 89 129
Hours: Mon–Sat, 8 am–5 pm.

Perennials, bulbs and lots of special plants for sale.

Specialist Suppliers

Some nurseries specialise in one type of plant only. The following nurseries have extensive collections of cottage specialties. Specialist plant societies (for example, for lilies, fuchsia, irises) are open to professional and amateur enthusiasts, and advertise in the 'Small Acorns' page of the *New Zealand Gardener*. This is also a marketplace for small gardeners with surplus stock for sale – worth checking for bargains and rarities.

Old Roses

Roseneath,
State Highway 1,
R.D. 2,
Albany. Tel: (09) 415 9204
Hours: Daily, 9 am–5.30 pm.

Seven km north of Albany. Over 1,000 varieties of old and classic roses – peak time November, through summer. Roses for sale. Admission charge. Bus tours must book.

Tasman Bay Roses,
Chamberlain Street North/P.O. Box 159,
Motueka. Tel: (0524) 87 449
Hours: Nursery, daily, 10 am–4.30 pm; Gardens, mid Nov–mid Jan; other times by arrangement.

More than 300 old and classic roses to choose from. Mail-order catalogue.

Paeonies

The Peony Gardens,
Lake Hayes,
No. 2 R.D.,
Queenstown. Tel: (03) 442 1210
Hours: Mid Nov–mid Dec (flowering season), or by arrangement.

Specialist producers of herbaceous and tree paeonies with 200 varieties displayed in the garden and nursery. No admission charge; send s.a.e. for free catalogue.

Tulips

Van Eeden Tulips,
West Plains,
R.D. 4,
Invercargill. Tel: (021) 57 836
Hours: Mid Oct–early Nov (flowering season), for public and for orders.

Full-colour catalogue, lovely selection. Catalogue sent out February; bulbs posted out April. Other bulbs include daffodils/narcissus, Spanish irises, crocuses, *Anemone blanda* (spring flowering), chionadoxa, puschkinia, and others.

Dianthus (Pinks)

The Homestead Nursery,
Mrs J. Marshall,
R.D. 1,
Darfield. Tel: (056) 88 335
Hours: May–Oct, Fri & Sat; other times by arrangement.

Herb Gardens

There are now several New Zealand nursery gardens specialising in herbs. Gardens which sell herbs as well as cottage flowers are noted above; well-established nurseries which specialise in herbs are listed below. Smaller specialist herb nurseries and gardens are listed in *Herbs in New Zealand*, published by the Herb Federation of New Zealand. Write to the Herb Federation (P.O. Box 33-007, Christchurch) for the current price of this booklet. *The Directory of Herbs in New Zealand* also contains contact addresses for herb societies, speakers on herbal topics and other information on how to increase your knowledge of herbs. It is well worth joining your local herb society if you want to improve this side of your cottage garden or make contact with a friendly circle of gardeners.

Don't forget, too, that many public and botanic gardens now feature a herb garden. The plants are usually labelled, and these are good places in which to start familiarising yourself with the wide range available. Public herb gardens of note can be found at the following:

• Silverdale Pioneer Herb Garden, Silverdale Historical Society Pioneer Village, Wainui Road, Silverdale.
• St Paul's Biblical Garden, St Paul's Anglican Church, Symonds Street, Auckland.
• Medicinal Herb Garden, Auckland Medical School, Grafton Road, Auckland. (Open at all times, tours by appointment.)
• Auckland Regional Botanic Garden, 102 Hill Road, Manurewa.
• Putaruru Timber Museum, State Highway 1, Putaruru. (Open Sun, Mon & Tues.)
• Tauranga Historical Village, Seventeenth Avenue, Tauranga. (Open daily, 9 am–4 pm; admission charge to village.)
• Arts Centre Complex, Cnr Dixon and Bruce Streets, Masterton.
• Wellington Botanic Gardens, Glenmore Street, Wellington.
• Mona Vale, Fendalton Road, Christchurch.
• Christchurch Botanic Gardens, Rolleston Avenue, Christchurch.
• Dunedin Botanic Gardens, Cnr Opoho and North Roads, Dunedin.
• Glenfalloch Woodland Gardens, Portobello Road, Otago Peninsula.

Auckland

Gilian Painter,
651 West Coast Road,
Oratia. Tel: (09) 818 5318
Hours: Daily, 9 am–5 pm; appointments preferred.
Unusual herbs and flowers from a leader of the 'herb revival' in New Zealand.

Aroha Cottage Herb Garden,
Jesmond Road,
R.D. 2, Drury. Tel: (09) 294 8659
Hours: Sat & Sun, 10 am–4 pm, or by appointment. Closed mid June–mid Aug.

Medieval-style herb garden, historic cottage, herbal products for sale. Devonshire teas and light lunches available.

Hawke's Bay

'Botany Way',
119 Meeanee Road,
Taradale. Tel: (070) 449 939
Hours: Appointments preferred.
Wide range of fragrant, medicinal and culinary herbs. Herbal medicines and creams made on the premises.

Weleda Garden,
Te Mata Peak Road/Box 132,
Havelock North. Tel: (070) 777 394
Hours: Mon–Fri, 9 am–5 pm.
Commercial cropping garden for the Weleda range of pure herbal products. Also plants and herbal products for sale. Appointments preferred, especially for tour groups.

Manawatu

Oranga Plants,
Port Street, off Pharazyn Street,
Feilding. Tel: (063) 34 233
Hours: Open daily; appointments preferred.
A herb nursery with display gardens and over 200 different herbs for sale.

Canterbury

Merrylea Cottage Herbs and Organic Gardens,
Coopers Creek,
Oxford. Tel: (0502) 24 489
Hours: Fri, Sat, Sun, 10 am–4 pm or by appointment. Shop open all year, gardens Oct–April.
Organic herbs grown for export. Herb plants, teas and cosmetics for sale.

The Herb Farm,
Rue Grehan,
Akaroa. Tel: (0514) 3575
Hours: Daily, 10 am–5 pm.
An acre of garden emphasising herbs in a beautiful bush setting. Herbs and herbal products for sale.

Otago

The Herb Nursery,
Cnr Double Hill and Main Roads,
Waititi. Tel: (024) 822 885
Hours: Aug–April, Thurs–Mon, 9 am–6 pm, and other times by arrangement.
Cottage and herb plants and herbal products for sale.
Organically grown vegetables for sale in spring and summer.

Seed Suppliers

Growing plants from seed is the cheapest way to establish a rich and varied cottage garden. It is also tremendously satisfying. Seeds vary enormously in size, shape and colour, and so do seed leaves and true leaves. If you are into cheap thrills, why not order a packet of unknown seed and watch to see what develops.

English garden books often list seed suppliers. For wild flower seeds, for example, see John Chambers' *Wild Flower Garden*. However, please remember that many foreign plants have become noxious weeds in New Zealand, and we don't need any more well-meaning but potentially destructive imports. So check a comprehensive reference book or consult with the Ministry of Agriculture and Fisheries or the DSIR Botany Division before ordering something unusual. Better still, stick to native plants for those out-of-the-ordinary touches in your garden (see below).

New Zealand

Grandma's Seeds,
South Head Road,
Parkhurst,
R.D. 1,
Helensville. Tel: (0880) 7312
Catalogue of old-fashioned annual and perennial seeds.

Kings Herb Seeds,
P.O. Box 19084/1660 Great North Road,
Avondale,
Auckland. Tel: (09) 887588
Sales from the shop, also a biennial colour catalogue with herbs, unusual flowers (especially flowers for drying), gourmet vegetables and essential oils. A must for thrifty gardeners.

Food Plant Resources,
S. Meadows,
194 Waimumu Road,
Massey,
Auckland 8.
Catalogue of unusual vegetable seeds.

Rainbow Seeds,
Box 5895,
Wellesley Street,
Auckland.
Rare and unusual seeds – mostly trees, but some vegetables and flowers.

Watkins Seeds,
P.O. Box 468,
New Plymouth. Tel: (067) 86800.
Colour catalogue with fancy varieties of popular flowers and interesting range of vegetable seeds.

England

Seeds can easily be ordered from England by quoting a credit card number or ordering a bank draft. Expect to pay around NZ$5 for a catalogue. Some seeds (e.g. *Nicotiana*) will be confiscated if your parcel is checked by the Ministry of Agriculture and Fisheries, so you might like to check with MAF before placing a large order.

Chiltern Seeds,
Bortree Stile,
Ulverston,
Cumbria LA127PB.

Mr Fothergills Seeds Ltd,
Kentford,
Newmarket,
Suffolk CB87BR.

Thompson and Morgan,
London Road,
Ipswich,
Suffolk IP20BA.

Unwins Seeds Ltd,
Histon,
Cambridge CB44LE.

Sutton's Seeds
This English seed supplier advertises in spring issues of the *New Zealand Gardener*. You can order the English catalogue with prices including post and packaging from England to New Zealand from P.O. Box 2918, Christchurch.

Native Plant Suppliers

The West Coast of the South Island is the last refuge of our native forests, and it also has a high concentration of native plant nurseries. There are native nurseries at Inangahua (on the main road north of Inangahua Junction), at Millerton (30 km north of Westport), and inland from Greymouth (see below). However, there are also excellent nurseries in other parts of New Zealand. I particularly envy Aucklanders their access to Platt's at Albany – always worth a visit.

The following addresses are for mail-order sources of native plants. Check your Yellow Pages to see if there is a native plant nursery near you. Keep your eyes open on your travels and be prepared to leave the beaten track – native nurseries are sometimes as shy and retiring as bush flowers.

Talisman Nurseries Limited,
Ringawhiti Road, R.D.,
Otaki. Tel: (069) 45893
Hours: Tues–Sun, 9 am–5 pm.

A wide range of natives, from subtropicals to alpines and ferns, and specialising in threatened New Zealand plants. Extensive catalogue available.

Goldfield Nurseries Limited,
P.O. Box 401,
Greymouth. Tel: (02726) 526.

Take the road through Boddytown from Greymouth, heading through the Aorangi Scenic Reserve towards Marsden. Ferns, orchids and groundcovers for sale, as well as trees and shrubs. Catalogue available.

Southern Seeds,
The Vicarage,
Sheffield,
Canterbury. Tel: (0516) 38814.

Native seeds collected from the Southern Alps; many rare and special plants on the seed list.

IDENTIFICATION OF COTTAGE GARDEN PLANTS

Achillea declorans 'W. B. Child'

Achillea fillipendulina 'Coronation Gold'

Achillea Galaxy hybrid 'The Beacon'

Achillea Galaxy hybrid 'Salmon Beauty'

Achillea ptarmica 'The Pearl'

Achillea x *taygetea* 'Moonshine'

Agapanthus minor

Agapanthus praecox

Ageratum houstonianum

Agrimonia odorata

Ajuga reptans atropurpurea

Alchemilla mollis

Alstroemeria 'Walter Fleming'

Althaea rosea 'Cottage Black'

Alyssum saxatile

Anemone bracteata

Anemone x hybrida 'Semi Double'

Anemone narcissiflora

Anemone nemorosa

Anemone nemorosa 'Vestal'

Anemone ranunculoides

Angelica archangelica

Aquilegia 'Adelaide Addison'

Aquilegia akitensis

Aquilegia 'Cottage Black'

Aquilegia 'Munstead White'

Aquilegia 'Norah Barlow'

Aquilegia vulgaris Variegata

Armeria maritima

Asperula odorata

Asphodeline lutea

Aster novae-angliae 'Lucida'

Astrantia major

Astrantia major Rosea

Astrantia maxima

Aubrieta deltoidea Alba

Aubrieta 'Snow In Summer'

Bellis perennis 'Rob Roy'

Bellis perennis 'Staffordshire Pink'

Bomarea multiflora

Buphthalmum salicifolium 'Golden Beauty'

Calamintha grandiflora

Campanula glomerata

Campanula persicifolia 'Double Form'

Campanula persicifolia 'Fleur de Neige'

Campanula rotundifolia

Campanula trachelium Alba

Centaurea montana

Cephalaria tartarica

Chaenomeles japonica 'Falconnet Charlet'

Cheiranthus 'Covent Garden Red'

Cheiranthus 'Harpur Crewe'

Chelidonium majus Flora Pleno

Chrysanthemum frutescens

Chrysanthemum maximum 'Little Princess'

Chrysanthemum parthenium Flora Plena

Chrysanthemum rubellum

Clematis heracleifolia

Clematis macropetala Flora Plena

Clematis 'Serenata'

Clianthus puniceus

Colchichum autumnale

Commelina coelestis

Convallaria majalis

Convallaria majalis Rosea

Coreopsis grandiflora

Coreopsis verticulata

Corydalis cheilanthifolia

Corydalis ochroleuca

Cosmos atrosanguineus

Cosmos bipinnatus 'Pink Sensation'

Crambe cordifolia

Crataegus oxyacantha

Crepis incana

Crocosmia aurea

Crocosmia x *crocosmiiflora* 'Solfatare'

Crocosmia x *crocosmiiflora* 'Star of the East'

Crocus aureus

Crucianella stylosa

Cyclamen neapolitanum

Cynoglossum nervosum

Dactylorrhiza elata

Dahlia 'Edinburgh'

Dahlia imperialis

Delphinium Garden hybrid

Delphinium nudicaule

Dianthus barbatus Auricula Eyed

Dianthus barbatus Auricula Eyed
Double Form

Dianthus 'A. J. Macself'

Dianthus 'Betty'

Dianthus 'Brympton Red'

Dianthus 'Devon Castle'

Dianthus 'Grandad Cuff'

Dianthus 'Inchmerry'

Dianthus 'Isolde'

Dianthus 'London Lovely'

Dianthus 'Midnite Snow'

Dianthus 'Mrs Sinkins'

Dianthus 'Painted Lady'

Dianthus 'Red Velvet'

Dianthus 'Sam Barlow'

Dianthus 'Waithmans Beauty'

Diascia rigescens

Dicentra formosa

Dicentra formosa Alba

Dicentra formosa 'Boothmans var.'

Dicentra spectabilis Alba

Dictamnus albus

Digitalis ambigua

Digitalis 'Inverewe Apricot'

Digitalis lanata

Digitalis lutea

Digitalis lutea x purpurea

Digitalis x mertonensis

Dodecatheon meadia 'Red Wings'

Echinops sphaerocephalus

Endymion hispanicus

Epimedium youngianum

Erigeron tweedii

Eryngium planum

Erysimum 'Constant Cheer'

Erysimum 'Joy Gold'

Erysimum 'Moonlight'

Erythronium 'Pagoda'

Erythronium tuolumnense

Eupatorium purpureum

Euphorbia griffithii 'Fireglow'

Euphorbia polychroma

Filipendula rubra

Filipendula ulmaria Flore Pleno

Fritillaria imperialis Aurea

Fritillaria mealeagris Alba

Fuchsia magellanica

Fuchsia thymifolia

Gaillardia 'Croftway Yellow'

Galanthus nivalis

Galega officinalis

Galega officinalis Alba

Geranium 'Claridge Druce'

Geranium endressii

Geranium himalayense Flore Pleno

Geranium macrorrhizum Alba

Geranium maderense

Geranium pratense Plenum Caeruleum

Geranium pratense Striata

Geranium sanguineum

Geranium sanguineum Alba

Geranium sanguineum 'Lancastriense'

Geranium traversii

Geranium wallichianum

Geum chiloense 'Fire Opal'

Geum chiloense 'Lady Stratheden'

Geum rivale

Geum sibirica

Gunnera manicata

Gypsophila paniculata 'Bristol Fairy'

Gypsophila 'Pink Star'

Hacquetia epipactus

Hedysarum coronarium

Helenium 'Butterpat'

Helenium 'Red Wonder'

Helenium 'Waalstrand'

Helianthemum 'Ben Hope'

Helianthemum 'Mrs Earls Red'

Heliotropium peruvianum

Helleborus corsicus

Helleborus foetidus

Hemerocallis 'Alcazar'

Hemerocallis 'Kwanso Variegata'

Hepatica nobilis

Hepatica triloba

Hesperis matronalis

Heuchera americana

Hieracium aurantiacum

Houstonia caerulea

Hyssopus officinalis

Iberis pruitti

Inula 'Golden Beauty'

Inula hookeri

Iris chrysographes 'Black Form'

Iris delavayi

Iris japonica 'Fairyland'

Jovellana lilacina

Kalmia latifolia

Kerria japonica Flore Pleno

Lamium aureum

Lathyrus latifolius 'Pink Pearl'

Lathyrus nervosus

Lathyrus odoratus 'Painted Lady'

Lathyrus rotundifolius

Lavandula angustifolia Atropurpurea

Lavandula stoechas

Leucojum vernum

Lewisia cotyledon 'Sunset Strain'

Ligularia dentata

Lilium chalcedonicum

Lilium martagon

Lilium martagon Alba

Lilium pardalinum

Lilium regale

Lilium tigrinum

Lilium tigrinum Plenescens

Linaria purpurea 'Canon Went'

Linum perenne

Lithospermum 'Grace Ward'

Lobelia cardinalis 'Queen Victoria'

Lonicera tellemaniana

Lunaria biennis Alba

Lupinus polyphyllus 'Noble Maiden'

Lupinus polyphyllus 'The Pages'

Lychnis chalcedonica

Lychnis chalcedonica Salmonea

Lychnis coronaria Alba

Lychnis flos-jovis

Lysimachia punctata

Lythrum salicaria 'Fire Candle'

Lythrum salicaria 'Rose Queen'

Macleaya microcarpa

Meconopsis cambrica

Meconopsis cambrica 'Francis Perry'

Meconopsis regia

Meconopsis x sheldonii

Mertensia virginica

Mimulus 'Andean Nymph'

Monarda didyma 'Croftway Pink'

Monarda didyma 'Fire Beacon'

Monarda didyma Violacea

Muscari botryoides Album

Myosotidium hortensia

Myosotis sylvatica

Narcissus bulbicodium

Narcissus x *odorus* 'Campernelle Plenus'

Narcissus 'Old Cottage Double'

Narcissus 'Paperwhite'

Narcissus poeticus

Nepeta mussinii

Nicotiana langsdorfii

Omphalodes cappadocica

Onopordum acanthium

Pachysandra terminalis

Paeonia lactiflora 'Cheddar Gold'

Paeonia mlokosewitschii

Paeonia officinalis Alba Plena

Paeonia tenuifolia

Papaver orientale 'Perrys White'

Papaver orientale 'Princess Victoria Louise'

Papaver somniferum

Papaver somniferum Paeoniaeflorum

Paris polyphylla

Pelargonium Black Leaved 'Distinction'

Pelargonium Bronze and Gold Leaved 'Jubilee'

Pelargonium Gold Leaved 'Verona'

Pelargonium Golden Tri-Colour 'Mr Henry Cox'

Pelargonium Ivy Leaved 'Blue Peter'

Pelargonium 'Nosegay'

Pelargonium Rosebud 'Apple Blossom'

Pelargonium Scented Leaved 'Lady Scarborough'

Pelargonium Silver Leaved 'Mrs J. C. Mappin'

Pelargonium Silver Tri-Colour 'Mrs Burdette Coutts'

Pelargonium Unique 'Scarlet'

Pelargonium Zonal 'Queen of Denmark'

Penstemon gloxinioides

Penstemon x hybrida 'Pink Clouds'

Phlomis fruticosa

Phlox paniculata 'Branklyn'

Phlox paniculata 'Mary Fox'

Phlox paniculata 'Starfire'

Phygelius capensis Coccineus

Plantago major Rubrifolia

Plantago rosularis

Polemonium caeruleum Alba

Polemonium roseum

Polygonatum multiflorum x hybridum

Polygonatum odoratum 'Gilt Edge'

Polygonum bistorta 'Superbum'

Polygonum filiforme 'Painters Palette'

Potentilla 'Miss Wilmott'

Primula auricula 'Argus'

(photo: J. J. Wemyss-Cooke)

Primula auricula Double

Primula auricula 'George Lightbody'

(photo: Dr R. Newton)

Primula 'Barnhaven Doubles'

Primula denticulata

Primula Double Gold Laced

Primula elatior

Primula florindae

Primula garryard 'Guinevere'

Primula Gold Laced

Primula Hose in Hose Gold Laced

Primula Hose in Hose Vulgaris

Primula Jackanapes Form

Primula Jack in the Green

Primula 'Kinlough Beauty'

Primula 'Tawny Port'

Primula veris

Primula veris 'Red and Orange'

Primula vialli

Primula vulgaris Alba

Primula vulgaris 'Old Irish Blue'

Pulmonaria angustifolia

Pulmonaria officinalis

Pulmonaria saccharata

Pulmonaria saccharata Argentia

Pulsatilla vulgaris

Ranunculus bulbosus Pleniflorus

Ranunculus ficaria

Reseda odorata

Ribes sanguineum

Rodgersia henrici

Rosmarinus 'Miss Jessups Upright'

Rudbeckia hirta

Rudbeckia 'Nutmeg'

Ruta graveolens

Salvia officinalis

Salvia 'Red Dragon'

Salvia x *superba*

Sanguisorba obtusa

Saxifraga umbrosa 'London Pride'

Scabiosa atropurpurea

Scabiosa caucasica 'Clive Greaves'

Semiaquilegia ecalcerata

Sidalcea 'Mrs Alderson'

Sidalcea 'Rev Page Roberts'

Sidalcea 'Rose Queen'

Silene gallica

Silene vulgaris

Sisyrinchium bermudiana

Sisyrinchium grandiflorum

Smilacina stellata

Soldanella montana

Stachys lanata

Stachys macrantha

Symphytum grandiflorum

Symphytum rubrum

Symphytum x *uplandicum* Variegatum

Syringa Double 'Madame Lemoine'

Syringa vulgaris

Thalictrum aquilegiifolium Alba

Thalictrum dipterocarpum

Thalictrum dipterocarpum 'Hewitts Double'

Thermopsis mollis

Thermopsis montana

Trachelium caeruleum

Tricyrtis formosana

Tricyrtis latifolia

Trifolium nigra

Trillium chloropetalum

Trillium erectum Alba

Trollius europaeus

Uvularia grandiflora

Verbascum chaixii Alba

Verbascum olympicum

Verbascum 'Pink Domino'

Verbena 'Pink Parfait'

Veronica latifolia 'Royal Blue'

Veronica longifolia

Vinca minor 'Miss Jekyll'

Viola 'Ardross Gem'

Viola 'Arkwrights Ruby'

Viola 'Bambini'

Viola biflora

Viola 'Bowles Black'

Viola cornuta Alba

Viola elatior

Viola 'Freckles'

Viola hederacea

Viola 'Irish Molly'

Viola 'Jury's Variegated'

Viola labradorica

Viola 'Maggie Mott'

Viola odorata Alba

Viola odorata 'Coeur d'Alsace'

Viola odorata 'Florist's Pride'

Viola odorata Pink and White Bi-Colour

Viola parma 'Marie Louise'

Viola 'The Joker'

Viola tricolour

Viola x *wittrockiana* 'Red Wings'

Viola x *wittrockiana* 'Super Beaconsfield'

Viscaria vulgaris Splendens Plena

Wistaria sinensis

Wistaria sinensis Alba

Traditional English Cottage Plants

Names in bold type indicate species illustrated; x=multi-coloured.
*=Especially suited to warmer, wetter parts of New Zealand.
†=Not suited to warmer, wetter parts of New Zealand.

SCIENTIFIC NAME	COMMON NAME	COLOUR	PLANT TYPE					HEIGHT			SEASON				SUN			MOISTURE		
			Annual	Biennial	Perennial	Climber	Shrub/Tree	Under 30 cm	30–90 cm	Over 90 cm	Spring	Summer	Autumn	Winter	Full sun	Part sun	Shady	Dryish	Average	Wettish
Acanthus mollis	Bear's breeches	white			●					●	●				●	●			●	●
Achillea decolorans	Yarrow	white			●				●			●			●	●			●	
Achillea Galaxy hybrids		salmon pink			●				●		●				●				●	
Achillea filipendulia	Yarrow	yellow			●				●			●	●		●				●	
Achillea millefolium		pink, white			●				●			●	●		●	●			●	
Achillea ptarmica		white			●				●			●	●		●	●				
Achillea x taygetea		yellow			●				●			●			●			●	●	
Aconicum napellum	Monkshood	purple, blue			●					●		●				●			●	●
Acroclinium roseum (Helipterum roseum)	Immortelle	x	●						●			●	●		●			●	●	
Ageratum houstonianum	Floss flower	mauve	●						●			●			●					
Agrimonia odorata	Agrimony	yellow			●				●			●			●				●	
Ajuga reptans	Bugle	blue-mauve			●			●			●	●			●	●		●	●	
Alchemilla mollis	Ladies' mantle	yellow			●				●			●			●	●				
Allium moly	Moly	yellow			●				●			●			●			●		
Althaea rosea	Hollyhock	red, pink, white	●		●					●		●			●				●	
Alyssum maritima (Lobularia maritima)	Sweet alyssum	white			●			●			●	●			●				●	
Alyssum saxatile	Golden alyssum	yellow	●					●				●	●		●				●	
Amaranthus caudatus	Love-lies-bleeding	red	●							●		●	●		●	●			●	
Anchusa azurea		blue			●				●	●	●				●				●	
Anemone blanda	Windflower	white			●			●			●			●	●	●		●	●	
Anemone bracteata		x			●			●			●				●				●	●
Anemone coronaria		x			●			●	●		●	●			●				●	
Anemone japonica x hybrida*		white, pink			●				●	●		●	●		●	●	●		●	
Anemone nemorosa		x			●			●			●					●			●	●
Anemone ranunculoides		yellow			●			●			●				●	●				

SCIENTIFIC NAME	COMMON NAME	COLOUR	PLANT TYPE					HEIGHT			SEASON				SUN			MOISTURE		
			Annual	Biennial	Perennial	Climber	Shrub/Tree	Under 30 cm	30–90 cm	Over 90 cm	Spring	Summer	Autumn	Winter	Full sun	Part sun	Shady	Dryish	Average	Wettish
Anthemis tinctoria	Dyer's chamomile	yellow			•				•			•			•				•	
Antirrhinum majus	Snapdragon	x	•						•			•	•		•				•	
Angelica archangelica		green			•					•		•			•	•			•	•
Aquilegia akitensis		blue, white			•				•		•	•			•	•			•	•
*Aquilegia vulgaris	Columbine, Granny's bonnet	x			•				•		•	•			•	•			•	•
Arabis albida	Rock cress	white			•			•			•				•	•		•		
*Armeria maritima	Thrift, Sea pink	pink			•			•			•	•			•			•	•	
Asphodeline lutea		yellow			•				•		•	•			•			•	•	
Aster amellus	Starwort	blue	•						•			•	•		•				•	•
Aster x frikartii		mauve, blue			•				•			•	•		•				•	•
Aster novae-angliae	Michaelmas daisy	blue, pink			•				•				•		•					•
*Aster novae-belgii		mauve			•				•				•		•					•
Astrantia major	Masterwort	white			•				•			•	•		•	•			•	
Astrantia maxima		mauve			•				•			•	•		•	•			•	
Astrantia rosea		pink			•				•			•	•		•	•			•	
Aubrieta deltoidea	Aubrieta	purple			•			•			•				•			•		
Bellis perennis	Daisy	white, pink			•			•			•				•	•			•	
Bomarea multiflora		orange				•					•	•			•	•			•	
Bupthalmum salicifolium		yellow			•			•				•			•				•	
Calamintha grandiflora	Calamint	pink			•			•				•			•				•	
*Calendula officinalis	Pot marigold	yellow	•					•	•			•	•		•	•			•	
Callistephus chinensis	China aster	x	•						•			•	•		•	•			•	
*Caltha palustris	Marsh marigold, Kingcup	yellow			•			•			•				•					•
Campanula carpatica		blue			•			•				•			•				•	
*Campanula glomerata		blue			•				•			•			•				•	
Campanula medium	Canterbury bells	blue, pink, white	•						•	•		•			•				•	
*Campanula persicifolia		blue, white			•					•		•			•				•	
Campanula pyramidalis		white			•					•		•			•				•	
*Campanula rotundifolia	Harebell	blue			•			•	•			•			•				•	
*Campanula trachelium	Bats in the belfry	mauve, white			•				•			•			•				•	
Catananche caerulea		blue			•				•		•	•	•		•			•		
*Centaurea cyanus	Cornflower	blue	•						•		•	•			•			•	•	
Centaurea dealbata		pink			•				•			•			•			•		
Centaurea montana		blue			•				•			•			•			•		
Centranthus ruber	Red valerian	red, pink			•				•			•			•	•		•	•	

SCIENTIFIC NAME	COMMON NAME	COLOUR	Annual	Biennial	Perennial	Climber	Shrub/Tree	Under 30 cm	30–90 cm	Over 90 cm	Spring	Summer	Autumn	Winter	Full sun	Part sun	Shady	Dryish	Average	Wettish
					PLANT TYPE				HEIGHT			SEASON				SUN			MOISTURE	
Cephalaria tartarica	Yellow scabious	yellow			●				●			●			●				●	
Cerastium tomentosum	Snow-in-summer	white			●			●			●	●			●			●		
Cerinthe major	Honeywort	mauve	●					●	●		●	●	●		●			●	●	
Chaenomeles japonica	Japonica	pink, red, orange					●			●	●				●				●	
Cheiranthus cheiri	Wallflower	yellow, red		●					●		●	●			●			●		
Chelidonium majus	Greater celandine	yellow			●				●		●				●	●			●	
Chrysanthemum frutescens	Bush daisy	white, pink, yellow			●					●	●		●		●	●		●	●	
Chrysanthemum maximum	Shasta daisy	white			●					●		●	●		●	●			●	
Chrysanthemum parthenium	Feverfew	white			●			●			●	●	●		●				●	
Chrysanthemum rubellum	Chusan daisy				●			●				●	●		●				●	
Clematis heracleifolia		blue				●						●			●				●	
Clematis macropetala		purple				●		●				●			●				●	
Clematis 'Serenata'		lilac				●					●	●			●				●	
Colchichum autumnale		pink, white			●			●					●		●				●	
Commelina coelestis		blue			●				●			●			●				●	
Consolida ambigua	Larkspur	blue	●						●	●		●			●				●	
†**Convallaria majalis**	Lily of the valley	white			●			●			●				●	●			●	●
Coreopsis grandiflora	Tickseed	yellow			●			●				●			●				●	
Coreopsis verticulata		yellow			●			●				●			●				●	
Corydalis cheilanthifolia					●			●			●				●				●	
Corydalis lutea	Prince of Wales feathers	yellow, white			●			●			●				●				●	
Cosmos atrosanguineus			●						●			●	●		●			●	●	
Cosmos bipinnatus	Cosmos	pink, white	●						●			●	●		●			●	●	
Crambe cordifolia		white			●					●		●			●			●		
Crataegus oxyacantha	Hawthorn	white, pink					●			●	●	●			●				●	
Crepis incana		pink			●			●				●			●				●	
Crocosmia aurea		yellow			●				●			●	●		●	●		●	●	
Crocosmia x crocosmiiflora		yellow-orange			●				●			●	●		●			●	●	
Crocosmia Garden hybrids		yellow			●				●			●	●		●			●	●	
Crocus vernus		x			●			●			●			●	●				●	
Cyclamen neapolitanum		pink, white			●			●				●	●				●	●	●	
Cynoglossum nervosum		blue	●						●			●			●				●	
Cynoglossum officinale	Houndstongue	blue	●						●		●	●			●	●		●	●	
Dactylorrhiza elata		magenta			●				●		●	●			●	●			●	
Dahlia x hybrida	Dahlia	x			●				●	●		●			●				●	

SCIENTIFIC NAME	COMMON NAME	COLOUR	Annual	Biennial	Perennial	Climber	Shrub/Tree	Under 30 cm	30–90 cm	Over 90 cm	Spring	Summer	Autumn	Winter	Full sun	Part sun	Shady	Dryish	Average	Wettish
Dahlia imperialis	Tree dahlia	pink			•					•		•			•				•	•
Delphinium hybridum		blue, white			•					•	•				•				•	
Delphinium nudicaule		pink, red			•				•	•	•				•				•	
Dianthus barbatus	Sweet William	pink, red	•					•			•				•				•	
Dianthus caryophyllus	Pink	pink, white			•			•	•		•	•			•			•	•	
Dianthus gratianopolitanus	Cheddar pink	pink			•			•			•				•			•	•	
Dianthus nitidus		pink			•			•				•	•		•			•	•	
Dicentra formosa		pink			•				•		•	•			•	•			•	
Dicentra spectabilis	Bleeding heart	pink, white			•				•		•	•			•	•			•	
Dictamnus albus	Burning bush	white			•					•	•				•				•	
Dierama pulcherrimum	Wand flower, Fairy bells	pink, white			•					•	•				•	•		•	•	
Digitalis lanata	Foxglove	white, mauve			•				•	•		•			•	•			•	
Digitalis lutea		yellow			•				•	•		•			•	•			•	
Digitalis x mertonensis		pink			•				•	•		•			•	•			•	
Digitalis purpurea		mauve			•					•	•	•			•	•			•	
Dodecatheon meadia	Shooting star	pink, white, mauve			•			•			•				•	•	•		•	
Echinops ritro	Globe thistle	blue			•				•			•	•		•	•			•	
Echinops sphaerocephalus		white			•					•		•			•				•	
Endymion hispanicus	Spanish bluebell	blue			•			•			•				•				•	
Endymion non-scriptus	Bluebell	blue			•			•			•				•	•			•	
Epimedium youngianum		white			•			•			•				•	•	•		•	
Eranthis hyemalis	Winter aconite	yellow			•			•			•			•						•
Erigeron mucronata	Babies' tears	white			•			•				•	•		•				•	
Erigeron specious	Fleabane	mauve, blue			•			•	•			•			•				•	
Erigeron tweedii		mauve			•			•				•			•				•	
Eryngium maritimum	Sea holly	blue			•				•			•	•		•			•	•	
Eryngium planum		blue			•				•			•	•		•			•	•	
Erythronium dens-canis	Dogtooth violet	purple			•			•			•					•				•
Erythronium revolutum	Trout lily	white			•			•			•					•			•	
Erythronium tuolumnense		yellow			•			•				•			•	•			•	
Eupatorium purpureum	Joe Pye weed	mauve, pink			•					•		•			•	•			•	•
Euphorbia griffithii		orange			•				•		•	•			•				•	
Euphorbia polychroma		green			•				•		•	•			•				•	
Filipendula hexapetala	Meadowsweet	cream			•							•			•	•			•	•
Filipendula rubra		pink			•					•		•			•				•	•

SCIENTIFIC NAME	COMMON NAME	COLOUR	PLANT TYPE					HEIGHT			SEASON				SUN			MOISTURE		
			Annual	Biennial	Perennial	Climber	Shrub/Tree	Under 30 cm	30–90 cm	Over 90 cm	Spring	Summer	Autumn	Winter	Full sun	Part sun	Shady	Dryish	Average	Wettish
Filipendula ulmaria		pink, white			●					●		●			●	●			●	●
†*Fritillaria imperialis*	Crown imperial	orange, red, yellow			●				●	●	●				●	●			●	
Fritillaria mealeagris	Snakeshead	mauve, white			●				●		●				●	●				●
Fuchsia magellanica		red			●				●			●			●	●			●	
Fuchsia thymifolia		pink			●			●	●			●			●	●			●	
Gaillardia x grandiflora		yellow			●				●			●			●				●	
†*Galanthus nivalis*	Snowdrop	white			●			●			●					●	●		●	
Galega officinalis	Goat's rue	mauve			●					●		●			●				●	
Galega officinalis 'Alba'		white			●					●		●			●				●	
Geranium endressii		pink			●				●			●	●		●			●	●	
Geranium himalayense		blue			●			●			●	●			●	●			●	
Geranium macrorrhizum		mauve, white			●				●			●	●		●			●	●	
Geranium maderense		pink			●					●		●			●				●	
Geranium pratense		blue, mauve, white			●				●			●	●		●				●	
Geranium sanguineum		red			●				●			●	●		●				●	
Geranium wallichianum		blue			●			●			●				●				●	
Geum x borisii		orange, red			●			●	●			●			●	●			●	
Geum chiloense		orange, yellow, red			●				●		●	●			●				●	
Geum montanum		red			●			●				●			●	●			●	
Geum rivale		orange			●			●				●			●	●			●	●
Gypsophila paniculata		white, pink			●				●			●	●		●			●		
Hacquetia epipactus		green			●			●			●				●	●			●	
Helenium autumnale	Sneezewort	yellow, orange, red			●					●		●			●				●	
Helianthemum nummularium	Sun rose	pink, red, white, yellow			●			●	●		●	●	●		●			●	●	
*Helianthus annus	Sunflower	yellow	●							●		●			●			●		
Helichrysum bracteatum	Strawflower, Everlasting	yellow, red, pink, white	●						●			●	●		●			●	●	
Heliotropium peruvianum	Heliotrope, Cherry pie	mauve	●						●			●	●			●			●	
Helleborus corsicus		green			●				●	●				●		●			●	
Helleborus foetidus		green			●				●					●		●			●	
Helleborus niger		white, pink			●				●					●		●			●	
Helleborus orientalis		white			●				●					●		●			●	
*Hemerocallis fulva	Day lily	yellow, orange			●				●			●			●				●	
Hemerocallis 'Kwanso Variegata'		orange			●				●			●			●				●	
Hepatica nobilis		blue			●			●			●			●		●			●	
Hesperis matronalis	Sweet rocket	mauve		●					●			●			●	●			●	

SCIENTIFIC NAME	COMMON NAME	COLOUR	Annual	Biennial	Perennial	Climber	Shrub/Tree	Under 30 cm	30–90 cm	Over 90 cm	Spring	Summer	Autumn	Winter	Full sun	Part sun	Shady	Dryish	Average	Wettish
Hyacinthus hybrids	Hyacinth	blue, purple, white			•			•			•			•	•	•			•	
Iberis umbellata	Candytuft	white, pink	•					•			•	•			•			•	•	
Iberis sempervivens		white			•			•	•		•				•				•	
Inula 'Golden Beauty'		yellow			•				•			•			•				•	
Inula hookeri		yellow			•				•			•			•				•	
Iris chrysographes		black			•					•	•	•			•				•	
Iris delavayi		mauve			•				•		•	•				•			•	
Iris douglasiana		mauve			•				•		•	•			•				•	
Iris foetidissima	Stinking gladwyn	yellow			•				•		•	•			•	•			•	
Iris unguicularis (*Iris stylosa*)		blue			•				•					•	•			•		
*Jasminum nudiflorum		yellow			•					•			•		•				•	
*Jasminum officinale	Jasmine	white			•					•	•	•			•				•	
*Jasminum polyanthum		white			•					•	•	•			•				•	
Jovellana lilacina		mauve			•				•			•			•				•	
Kalmia latifolia		pink/white					•		•		•	•			•	•			•	
Kerria japonica		yellow					•		•		•	•			•	•			•	
*Lamium maculatum Garden varieties	Dead nettle	pink, white			•			•			•	•			•	•			•	
Lathyrus latifolius	Perennial pea	pink/white			•				•		•	•			•				•	
Lathyrus nervosus	Lord Anson's pea	mauve			•					•	•	•				•			•	
*Lathyrus odoratus	Sweet pea	x	•								•	•	•		•	•			•	
Lathyrus rotundifolius		red			•				•	•	•				•				•	
*Lavatera trimestris		pink	•						•	•	•	•	•		•				•	
*Lavandula angustifolia	Lavender	mauve			•				•			•			•			•	•	
Lavandula dentata		mauve			•				•	•		•			•			•	•	
*Lavandula spica		mauve, white, pink			•				•			•			•			•	•	
*Lavandula stoechas		mauve			•				•	•	•				•			•	•	
Leucojum vernum	Snowflake	white			•			•	•		•			•	•			•		•
Lewisia cotyledon		white/orange	•					•			•				•			•	•	
Ligularia denticulata		yellow, orange			•					•		•			•	•			•	•
*Lilium candidum	Madonna lily	white			•				•			•			•	•			•	
*Lilium chalcedonicum	Turk's cap	orange			•				•			•			•	•			•	
*Lilium martagon		pink			•					•		•			•	•			•	
*Lilium martagon 'Alba'		white			•					•		•			•	•			•	
*Lilium pardalinum	Leopard lily	red, yellow			•					•		•			•	•			•	
*Lilium regale	Christmas lily	white			•				•			•			•	•			•	

SCIENTIFIC NAME	COMMON NAME	COLOUR	Annual	Biennial	Perennial	Climber	Shrub/Tree	Under 30 cm	30–90 cm	Over 90 cm	Spring	Summer	Autumn	Winter	Full sun	Part sun	Shady	Dryish	Average	Wettish
*Lilium tigrinum	Tiger lily	orange			●					●		●			●	●			●	
Limnanthes douglasii	Poached egg plant, Meadowfoam	white/yellow	●					●			●	●			●				●	
*Limonium latifolium	Sea lavender	mauve, white			●				●			●			●				●	
*Linaria maroccana		x			●				●			●			●				●	
*Linaria purpurea	Toadflax	mauve, pink			●				●			●	●		●			●		
*Linum perenne	Flax	blue, white			●				●			●			●				●	
Lithospermum 'Grace Ward'		blue			●			●				●			●				●	
*Lobelia cardinalis	Cardinal flower	red			●				●	●		●	●		●				●	
Lonicera spp.	Honeysuckle	yellow, white				●				●	●	●			●	●			●	
Lonicera tellemaniana		orange				●				●	●	●			●	●			●	
*Lunaria biennis	Honesty	mauve, white		●					●		●				●	●			●	
*Lupinus polyphyllus	Lupin	x			●					●	●	●			●	●		●	●	
*Lychnis chalcedonica	Maltese cross	red			●				●			●			●				●	
Lychnis coronaria	Rose campion	pink			●				●			●			●				●	
Lychnis coronaria 'Alba'		white			●				●			●			●				●	
*Lychnis flos-cuculi	Cuckoo flower	pink, white			●			●			●	●			●				●	
*Lychnis flos-jovis	Flower of Jove	pink			●			●	●		●	●			●				●	
Lysimachia nummularia	Creeping Jenny	yellow			●			●				●			●		●		●	●
*Lysimachia punctata		yellow			●				●			●			●				●	●
*Lythrum salicaria	Loosestrife	purple, pink			●				●			●	●		●	●				●
Macleaya microcarpa	Plume poppy	red			●					●	●	●			●			●	●	
Malcolmia maritima	Virginia stock	mauve, pink	●					●	●		●	●			●				●	
Malus floribunda	Crab apple	white, pink					●			●	●				●	●		●	●	
Malva alcea	Mallow	pink			●				●	●		●	●		●			●		
Matthiola bicornis	Night-scented stock	mauve	●						●		●	●			●				●	
Meconopsis cambrica	Welsh poppy	yellow, orange			●			●	●		●	●			●	●			●	
Meconopsis regia		yellow			●					●		●			●	●			●	
Meconopsis x sheldonii		blue			●					●	●	●			●	●			●	
Mirabilis jalapa	Marvel of Peru	yellow/red			●				●			●	●		●				●	
Monarda didyma	Sweet bergamot	red, pink, purple			●				●	●		●			●	●			●	●
Muscari botryoides	Grape hyacinth	blue, white			●			●			●				●				●	
Myosotis sylvatica	Forget-me-not	blue		●				●			●				●				●	
Narcissus bulbicodium	Hoop petticoat daffodil	yellow			●			●			●				●				●	
Narcissus 'Old Cottage Double'		yellow			●			●			●				●				●	
Narcissus x odorus 'Campernelle'	Queen Anne's Irish campernelle	yellow			●			●			●				●				●	

SCIENTIFIC NAME	COMMON NAME	COLOUR	Annual	Biennial	Perennial	Climber	Shrub/Tree	Under 30 cm	30–90 cm	Over 90 cm	Spring	Summer	Autumn	Winter	Full sun	Part sun	Shady	Dryish	Average	Wettish
Narcissus poeticus		yellow, white			•			•			•				•				•	
Nepeta mussinii	Catmint	blue			•			•				•			•				•	
*Nicotiana alata	Tobacco flower	white			•				•			•	•		•	•			•	
Nicotiana langsdorfii		green, red			•				•		•	•			•				•	
*Nigella damascena	Love-in-a-mist	blue, white	•						•			•			•	•			•	
*Oenothera biennis	Evening primrose	yellow			•				•			•			•			•		
*Omphalodes cappadocia	Blue-eyed Betty	blue			•			•			•	•				•			•	•
Omphalodes verna	Blue-eyed Mary	blue			•			•			•					•	•			
Onoopordum acanthium		white			•					•		•			•			•	•	
*Ornithogalum umbellatum	Star of Bethlehem	white			•				•		•				•	•			•	
Pachysandra terminalis		white			•			•			•			•	•	•	•		•	
†**Paeonia lactiflora**	Paeony	red, pink white			•				•		•				•	•			•	
Paeonia mlokosewitschii		yellow			•				•		•				•	•			•	
†**Paeonia officinalis**		red, white			•				•		•				•	•			•	
Paeonia tenuifolia		red			•				•		•				•	•			•	
Papaver orientale	Oriental poppy	red			•					•	•				•				•	
*Papaver rhoeas	Shirley poppy	red, pink	•						•		•	•			•	•			•	
Papaver somniferum	Opium poppy	white, red			•				•	•	•				•				•	
*Pelargonium x domesticum	Geranium	red, pink, white			•				•		•	•			•	•			•	
*Penstemon gloxinioides		red, blue, mauve			•				•		•	•			•				•	
Penstemon x hybrida		x			•				•		•				•			•	•	
Phlomis fruticosa	Jerusalem sage	yellow			•				•		•				•			•	•	
*Phlox maculata		pink, white			•				•	•	•					•			•	
*Phlox paniculata		pink, white			•				•	•					•				•	
*Polemonium caeruleum	Jacob's ladder	mauve, blue			•				•		•	•			•	•			•	•
Polygonatum x hybridum	Solomon's seal	white			•				•		•						•		•	
Polygonum bistorta	Bistort	pink			•				•			•			•				•	
*Polygonum vaccinifolium	Knotweed	pink			•			•				•	•		•				•	
Potentilla atrosanguinea		red-yellow			•			•	•		•	•			•				•	
Primula auricula	Dusty miller	x			•			•	•		•				•	•			•	
*Primula hybrid	Polyanthus	x			•			•			•				•	•			•	
Primula veris	Cowslip	yellow			•			•			•				•	•			•	
*Primula vulgaris	Primrose	yellow, white			•			•			•				•	•			•	
*Prunella webbiana	Self heal	mauve			•			•				•			•	•			•	
*Pulmonaria angustifolia	Lungwort	blue/pink			•			•			•					•	•		•	

SCIENTIFIC NAME	COMMON NAME	COLOUR	Annual	Biennial	Perennial	Climber	Shrub/Tree	Under 30 cm	30–90 cm	Over 90 cm	Spring	Summer	Autumn	Winter	Full sun	Part sun	Shady	Dryish	Average	Wettish
Pulsatilla vulgaris	Pasque flower	purple			●			●			●				●				●	
Ranunculus asiaticus		red, yellow, orange			●				●		●				●				●	
Reseda odorata	Mignonette	yellow	●						●			●	●		●				●	
Ribes sanguineum	Flowering currant	pink					●			●	●				●	●			●	
Rodgersia henrici		pink			●					●	●	●			●	●			●	●
Rosa spp. (see 'Cottage Roses', Appendix IV) **Rosmarinus officinalis**	Rosemary	blue					●		●	●		●			●				●	
***Rudbeckia hirta**		yellow			●				●			●	●		●				●	
Ruta graveolens	Rue	yellow			●				●			●			●				●	
Salvia officinalis	Sage	blue			●				●		●	●			●			●	●	
***Salvia patens*		blue			●				●			●			●				●	
***Salvia x superba**		blue, red			●				●			●			●				●	
Sanguisorba obtusa		pink			●					●		●			●	●				●
***Saponaria officinalis*	Soapwort	pink			●				●	●		●	●		●	●			●	
Saxifraga umbrosa	London pride	pink			●				●		●	●				●			●	
Scabiosa atropurpurea	Scabious	magenta			●				●			●	●		●			●		
***Scabiosa caucasia**	Scabious, Pin cushion flower	mauve, white			●				●			●	●		●			●	●	
Sedum acre	Biting stonecrop	yellow			●			●				●			●			●		
Semiaquilegia ecalcerata		mauve			●			●			●	●				●	●		●	
Sidalcea malviflora		pink, white			●				●			●			●				●	
Silene gallica		red			●				●			●			●				●	
***Silene maritima*	Sea campion	white, pink			●			●			●				●	●			●	
Sisyrinchium bermudiana		blue			●			●				●			●			●	●	
Sisyrinchium grandiflorum		yellow			●			●				●			●			●	●	
***Solidago canadensis*	Golden rod	yellow			●					●		●	●		●	●			●	
***Stachys lanata**	Lamb's lugs	white			●			●	●			●			●				●	
Stachys macrantha		pink			●			●				●			●	●			●	
Stokesia laevis	Stoke's aster	blue			●				●			●	●		●				●	
Symphoricarpus rivularis	Snowberry	white (berries)					●			●			●						●	
Symphytum grandiflorum		cream			●			●			●	●			●	●			●	
Symphytum rubrum		red			●				●		●	●				●			●	
***Symphytum x uplandicum**		blue			●				●		●	●				●			●	
Syringa vulgaris	Lilac	purple, white					●			●	●				●				●	
Thalictrum aquilegiifolium	Meadow rue	mauve, pink			●				●	●	●	●			●				●	
Thalictrum dipterocarpum		mauve			●					●		●			●	●			●	

SCIENTIFIC NAME	COMMON NAME	COLOUR	PLANT TYPE					HEIGHT			SEASON				SUN			MOISTURE		
			Annual	Biennial	Perennial	Climber	Shrub/Tree	Under 30 cm	30–90 cm	Over 90 cm	Spring	Summer	Autumn	Winter	Full sun	Part sun	Shady	Dryish	Average	Wettish
Thalictrum flavum		yellow			•				•	•		•			•	•			•	
Thermopsis mollis		yellow			•					•	•	•			•				•	
Thermopsis montana		yellow			•					•	•	•			•				•	
Tradescantia virginiana	Spiderwort	blue			•				•		•	•	•		•	•			•	
Tricyrtis formosana	Toad lily	red			•				•			•			•	•			•	
Tricyrtis latifolia		blue			•				•			•			•	•			•	
Trifolium nigra	Black clover	black (leaves)			•			•			•			•	•	•	•	•	•	•
Trillium chloropetalum		white, red			•			•			•				•	•	•		•	
Trillium erectum	Trinity flower	white, red			•			•			•				•	•	•		•	
Trollius europaeus	Globe flower	yellow			•				•		•	•			•	•			•	•
Tropaeleum majus	Nasturtium	red, yellow	•					•				•	•		•	•			•	
Tulipa 'Cottage Tulips'	Tulip	x			•				•		•				•				•	
Tulipa gesneriana major		red			•				•		•				•				•	
Uvularia grandiflora		yellow			•				•		•					•	•		•	
Verbascum chaiaxii	Mullein	yellow			•				•				•		•			•	•	
Verbascum chaiaxii 'Alba'		white			•					•			•		•			•	•	
Verbascum olympicum		yellow			•					•		•			•			•	•	
Verbascum phoeniceum		x			•					•		•			•			•	•	
Veronica latifolia		blue			•			•				•			•	•			•	
Veronica longifolia		blue			•				•			•			•	•			•	
Veronica spicata	Speedwell	blue			•				•		•	•			•	•			•	
Vinca major	Greater periwinkle	blue, white			•			•			•	•	•			•	•	•	•	
Vinca minor	Lesser periwinkle	blue, white			•			•			•	•	•			•	•		•	
Viola canina	Dog violet	purple			•			•			•					•	•		•	
Viola cornuta	Horned violet	white, mauve			•			•				•			•	•			•	
Viola odorata	Violet	purple, white			•			•			•				•	•			•	
Viola x wittrockiana	Pansy	pink, x	•					•			•	•	•		•	•			•	

COTTAGEY NEWCOMERS

SCIENTIFIC NAME	COMMON NAME	COLOUR	PLANT TYPE					HEIGHT			SEASON				SUN			MOISTURE		
			Annual	Biennial	Perennial	Climber	Shrub/Tree	Under 30 cm	30–90 cm	Over 90 cm	Spring	Summer	Autumn	Winter	Full sun	Part sun	Shady	Dryish	Average	Wettish
Agapanthus praecox (*A. umbellatus*)		blue, white			●				●	●	●	●			●				●	
Alstroemeria ligtu (*A. pulchella*)	Peruvian lily	pink, red			●				●		●	●	●		●	●			●	
Amaryllis belladonna	Naked ladies, Belladonna lily	pink, white			●				●			●	●		●			●		
Anaphalis yedoensis	Pearly everlasting	white			●			●				●	●		●			●		
Aruncus dioicus	Goat's beard	white			●					●		●				●				●
Astilbe x arendsii		white, pink			●				●			●				●				●
Bergenia cordifolia		pink			●			●	●		●			●				●	●	●
Brachycome multifidia (*B. ciliaris*)	Swan River daisy	blue, mauve			●				●			●	●		●			●	●	
Browallia speciosa	Bush violet	blue, mauve	●						●			●	●			●			●	
Brunnera macrophylla		blue			●				●		●	●				●	●		●	●
Canna indica (*C. lutea*)	Canna lily	red, yellow			●					●		●	●		●	●				●
Cassiope tetragona		white			●			●			●					●			●	●
Ceratostigma willmotianum		blue			●				●			●	●		●				●	
Colchicum speciosum	Autumn crocus	mauve, white			●			●					●			●			●	
Convolvulus cneorum		white			●			●	●		●	●	●		●			●		
Convolvulus mauritanica		mauve			●			●	●		●	●			●			●		
Coreopsis auriculata					●				●			●	●		●			●	●	
Coreopsis tinctoria		red			●			●				●	●		●			●		
Daboecia cantabrica	St Daboec's heath	white, pink			●				●			●	●		●				●	
Diascia cordata		pink			●			●				●	●		●			●	●	
Dictamnus fraxinella		white			●				●			●			●			●		
Dimorphotheca ecklonis		white			●			●	●		●	●			●			●	●	
Doronicum plantagineum	Leopard's bane	yellow			●				●		●	●			●	●				●
Echinacea purpurea	Purple coneflower	purple			●				●			●	●		●			●	●	
Echium plantagineum		blue, mauve, pink	●						●			●			●			●		

SCIENTIFIC NAME	COMMON NAME	COLOUR	Annual	Biennial	Perennial	Climber	Shrub/Tree	Under 30 cm	30–90 cm	Over 90 cm	Spring	Summer	Autumn	Winter	Full sun	Part sun	Shady	Dryish	Average	Wettish
Epimedium spp.		white			●				●		●				●	●			●	
Eschscholzia californica	Californian poppy	yellow, white	●					●			●	●			●			●		
Euphorbia wulfenii		yellow/green			●				●	●	●				●			●	●	
Felicia amelloides		blue			●			●	●			●	●		●				●	
Felicia gracilis		mauve			●			●	●			●	●		●				●	
Francoa sonchifolia	Bridal veil	white			●				●	●		●	●		●	●		●	●	
Freesia refracta		white, yellow			●			●			●				●	●			●	
Gaillardia pulchella		red/yellow			●			●				●	●		●			●		
Galtonia candicans	Cape hyacinth	white			●					●		●	●		●			●	●	
Gaura lindheimeri		white			●				●		●	●	●		●				●	
Gladiolus nanus		x			●			●	●		●	●			●				●	
Hardenbergia violaceae		mauve				●					●	●			●	●			●	
Heliopsis helanthiodes		yellow			●				●	●		●	●		●				●	●
Heuchera sanguinea	Coral bells	pink			●				●			●	●		●	●			●	
Hosta spp.	Plantain lily	white, mauve			●				●				●			●			●	●
Kniphofia (varieties)	Red hot poker	red, pink			●					●		●	●		●				●	
Lewisia (varieties)		red, pink			●			●			●	●			●			●	●	
Liatris spicata	Gayfeather	mauve			●				●			●	●		●				●	
Liriope muscari		purple			●			●	●			●	●		●	●		●	●	
Lithospermum diffusum		blue			●			●				●			●			●	●	
Lysimachia clethroides		white			●				●			●	●		●	●				●
Mandevillea suaveolens	Chilean jasmine	white				●				●		●	●		●	●			●	
Nierembergia repens		white			●			●				●				●			●	
Nierembergia rivularis		white			●			●				●				●			●	
Pandorea pandorana	Wongawonga vine	white				●					●	●			●				●	
Parthenocissus quinquefolia	Virginia creeper	red				●				●			●		●	●			●	
Passiflora mollisima	Banana passionfruit	pink				●				●		●			●	●			●	
Phlomis russeliana		yellow			●				●				●			●		●	●	
Potentilla fructicosa		yellow			●				●			●	●		●	●		●	●	
Rhodohypoxis baueri		pink, white			●			●			●	●	●		●				●	
Rodgersia pinnata		pink			●				●	●		●				●				●
Rudbeckia fulgida	Coneflower	yellow			●				●			●	●		●	●				●
Saponaria ocymoides	Rock soapwort	pink			●			●	●		●				●				●	
Sedum spectabile		pink			●				●				●		●			●	●	
Solanum jasminoides (*S. wendlandi*)	Potato vine	white, mauve				●				●		●			●				●	

SCIENTIFIC NAME	COMMON NAME	COLOUR	PLANT TYPE					HEIGHT			SEASON				SUN			MOISTURE		
			Annual	Biennial	Perennial	Climber	Shrub/Tree	Under 30 cm	30–90 cm	Over 90 cm	Spring	Summer	Autumn	Winter	Full sun	Part sun	Shady	Dryish	Average	Wettish
Stephanotis floribunda		white				•			•	•		•			•	•			•	
Sternbergia lutea	Autumn crocus	yellow			•			•					•		•	•		•	•	
Thunbergia alata	Black-eyed Susan	orange, yellow	•			•				•		•	•		•				•	
Tiarella cordifolia	Foam flower	white			•			•			•	•				•	•		•	•
Trachelium caeruleum		mauve			•				•			•			•	•			•	
Trillium grandiflorum	Wake Robin	white			•			•	•		•					•			•	
Tropaeolum speciosum	Flame flower	red				•				•		•			•	•			•	
Vitis coignetiae	Crimson glory vine	red, yellow				•				•			•		•	•		•	•	
Vitis vinifera	Ornamental grape	yellow, red				•				•			•		•				•	
Wistaria sinensis		white, mauve				•				•	•	•			•			•		

NEW ZEALAND COTTAGE PLANTS

Where no colours or seasons are given the plant is grown primarily for foliage, or for medicinal purposes. Where no height is given (for shrubs or trees) check mature height before planting. This list is a selection of suitable native plants only, and reference should be made to a book on native plants for other alternatives.

SCIENTIFIC NAME	COMMON NAME	COLOUR	PLANT TYPE					HEIGHT			SEASON				SUN			MOISTURE		
			Annual	Biennial	Perennial	Climber	Shrub/Tree	Under 30 cm	30–90 cm	Over 90 cm	Spring	Summer	Autumn	Winter	Full sun	Part sun	Shady	Dryish	Average	Wettish
Acaena caesiiglauca	Piripiri, Bidibid	blue-grey foliage			●			●							●			●	●	
Acaena microphylla	Piripiri, Bidibid	red-brown foliage			●			●							●			●	●	
Acaena novae-zealandiae	Piripiri, Bidibid	red foliage			●			●							●			●	●	
Aciphylla aurea	Golden Spaniard	white			●					●		●			●			●	●	
Alectryon excelsum	Titoki	red-black fruit					●						●		●	●			●	
Alseuosmia macrophylla	Toropapa	red					●				●	●				●			●	
Anisotome aromatica		white						●			●				●			●	●	
Apium australe	Wild celery		●					●							●				●	
Aristotelia serrata	Makomako, Wineberry	white, purple berries					●				●		●		●				●	
Arthropodium cirratum	Rengarenga lily	white			●				●			●			●	●			●	
Arthropodium candidum		white			●			●				●			●	●			●	
Ascarina lucida	Hutu						●								●	●			●	
Brachyglottis repanda	Rangiora	white					●				●	●			●	●			●	
Bulbinella angustifolia	Maori onion	yellow			●				●			●			●				●	●
Bulbinella hookeri	Maori onion	yellow			●				●			●			●				●	●
Carpodetus serratus	Putaputaweta, Marbleleaf	white					●					●			●	●			●	
Celmisia gracilenta	Pekepeke	white			●			●	●		●				●				●	
Celmisia mackaui		white			●			●				●			●	●		●	●	
Celmisia petiolata		white			●			●				●				●			●	
Celmisia spectabilis	Puharetaiko	white			●			●				●			●			●	●	
Clematis paniculata	Puawananga	white				●				●	●						●			●	
Clianthus puniceus	Kakabeak	pink, red, white					●				●	●			●				●	
Coprosma grandifolia	Manono						●									●			●	
Coprosma repens	Taupata						●									●			●	
Coprosma robusta	Karamu	orange berries					●						●		●	●			●	

SCIENTIFIC NAME	COMMON NAME	COLOUR	PLANT TYPE					HEIGHT			SEASON				SUN			MOISTURE		
			Annual	Biennial	Perennial	Climber	Shrub/Tree	Under 30 cm	30–90 cm	Over 90 cm	Spring	Summer	Autumn	Winter	Full sun	Part sun	Shady	Dryish	Average	Wettish
Cordyline australis	Ti, Cabbage tree	white					●				●				●			●	●	
Cordyline banksii	Ti ngahere	white					●				●					●			●	
Cordyline indivisa	Toii	white					●				●					●			●	
Corokia buddleioides							●								●	●			●	
Corokia cotoneaster	Korokio	yellow					●								●				●	
Corokia x *virgata*							●								●				●	
Corynocarpus laevigatis	Karaka	orange fruit					●						●		●				●	
Cotula pyrethrifolia		white			●			●				●			●				●	
Cotula squalida		yellow			●			●				●			●				●	
Craspedia uniflora	Woollyhead	white, yellow			●				●				●		●		●	●	●	
Dianella nigra	Turutu	blue berries			●				●			●			●	●			●	
Dodonea viscosa	Ake ake	red					●				●	●			●				●	
Dodonea var. *purpurea*		purple					●								●				●	
Elaeocarpus dentatus	Hinau	white					●				●				●	●			●	
Entelea arborescens	Whau	white					●				●				●				●	
Euphrasia cuneata	Tutumako, NZ Eyebright	white			●			●				●			●	●		●	●	●
Fuchsia excorticata	Kotukutuku	purple					●				●				●	●			●	
Fuchsia procumbens		red-purple berries			●			●			●				●	●			●	
Gentiana astonii	Cliff gentian	white			●			●				●			●	●		●	●	
Gentiana saxosa	Shore gentian	white			●			●					●		●				●	
Gaultheria colensoi	Snowberry	white					●				●			●				●	●	
Gaultheria crassa		white					●				●			●				●	●	
Geranium microphyllum		white			●			●				●			●			●		
Geranium traversii		pink			●			●			●	●			●				●	
Geum urbanum var. *strictum*	Kopata, Avens	yellow			●			●				●			●				●	
Gingidia montana	Maori anise	white			●			●				●			●				●	●
Gnaphalium keriense	Puatea	white			●			●			●	●			●		●	●		
Gunnera dentata		red foliage			●			●									●		●	
Hebe albicans		white					●					●			●				●	
Hebe diosmifolia		white, mauve					●					●			●				●	
Hebe hartii		mauve					●					●			●				●	
Hebe hulkeana		mauve					●				●				●				●	
Hebe parviflora		white					●					●			●				●	
Hebe salicifolia	Koromiko	white					●					●			●				●	
Hebe speciosa	Napuka	red, purple					●					●	●		●				●	

SCIENTIFIC NAME	COMMON NAME	COLOUR	Annual	Biennial	Perennial	Climber	Shrub/Tree	Under 30 cm	30–90 cm	Over 90 cm	Spring	Summer	Autumn	Winter	Full sun	Part sun	Shady	Dryish	Average	Wettish
Hebe townsonii		white					•	•			•				•				•	
Helichrysum bellidioides		white			•			•				•			•				•	
Hibiscus trionum		yellow	•						•			•	•		•				•	
Hoheria lyallii	Houhi, Mountain lacebark	white					•					•			•	•			•	
Hoheria populnea	Houhere	white					•					•			•	•		•	•	
Jovellana sinclairii	Maori calceolaria	white			•			•			•	•			•				•	•
Kunzea ericoides	Kanuka	white					•	•			•				•	•			•	
Lepidium oleraceum	Nau, Cook's scurvy grass				•			•				•			•				•	
Leptospermum scoparium	Manuka	white, red, pink					•	•			•	•			•				•	
Leucogenes grandiceps	Sth Island edelweiss	white			•			•			•	•			•				•	
Leucogenes leontopodium	Nth Island edelweiss	white			•			•			•	•			•				•	
Libertia ixioides	Mikoikoi, NZ iris	white, orange berries			•			•	•		•		•		•	•			•	
Libocedrus bidwillii	Pahautea, NZ cedar									•					•	•			•	
Libocedrus plumosa	Kawaka									•					•	•			•	
Linum monogynum	Rauhuia	white			•			•			•	•			•				•	
Lophomyrtus bullata	Ramarama						•				•	•			•				•	
Macropiper excelsum	Kawakawa						•					•	•		•	•			•	
Mazus radicans	Swamp musk	white			•			•			•	•			•					•
Melicope ternata	Wharangi						•					•			•	•			•	
Melicytus ramiflorus	Mahoe, Whiteywood	green					•				•	•			•	•			•	
Mentha cunninghamii	Hioi, Native mint				•			•				•			•				•	
Metrosideros carminea	Crimson rata	red				•					•	•			•				•	
Metrosideros excelsa	Pohutukawa	red				•						•			•			•	•	
Myosotidium hortensia	Chatham Island forget-me-not	blue			•			•	•			•				•			•	•
Myosotis eximia		white			•			•				•			•				•	
Myosotis explanata	Arthur's Pass forget-me-not	white			•			•				•			•	•			•	
Myosotis macrantha		yellow			•			•				•			•				•	
Nertera depressa	Common nertera	red berries			•			•				•	•			•				•
Nothofagus fusca	Tawhairaunui, Red beech						•								•	•			•	
Olearia albida		white					•					•	•		•				•	
Olearia arborescens	Common tree daisy	white					•				•	•			•				•	
Olearia avicenniaefolia		white					•				•	•			•	•			•	
Olearia cheesemanii	Stream-side daisy	white					•				•	•			•				•	•
Olearia paniculata	Akiraho	white					•				•	•			•			•	•	
Olearia rani	Heketara	white					•				•					•			•	

SCIENTIFIC NAME	COMMON NAME	COLOUR	Annual	Biennial	Perennial	Climber	Shrub/Tree	Under 30 cm	30–90 cm	Over 90 cm	Spring	Summer	Autumn	Winter	Full sun	Part sun	Shady	Dryish	Average	Wettish
Olearia traversii	Chatham Island ake ake						•								•			•	•	
Ourisia caespitosa		white			•			•				•			•	•			•	•
Ourisia macrophylla		white			•				•		•	•				•			•	•
Pachystegia insignis	Marlborough daisy	white			•				•			•			•			•	•	
Parahebe catarractae		white, mauve			•			•				•			•	•			•	•
Parahebe lyallii		white, mauve			•			•				•	•		•	•			•	•
Parsonsia capsularis	Akakiore, Maori jasmine	white				•					•	•				•			•	
Parsonsia heterophylla	Kaiku, Maori jasmine	white				•					•	•	•			•			•	
Pennantia corymbosa	Kaikomako	white					•					•			•	•			•	
Phormium tenax	Harakeke, NZ flax	red				•				•	•	•			•				•	•
Pimelea prostrata	Pinatoro	white					•	•			•	•			•			•	•	
Pittosporum crassifolium	Karo	purple					•					•			•			•	•	
Pittosporum eugenioides	Tarata, Lemonwood	yellow					•				•				•	•			•	
Pittosporum tenuifolium	Kohuhu	purple					•				•				•				•	
Podocarpus totara var. *aureus*	Golden totara						•								•				•	
Pomaderris kumerahou	Golden tainui	yellow					•				•	•			•	•			•	
Pratia angulata		white			•			•			•	•				•			•	•
Pseudopanax crassifolius	Horoeka, Lancewood						•								•				•	
Pseudopanax discolor							•								•	•			•	
Pseudopanax lessonii	Houpara						•								•	•			•	
Pseudowintera colorata	Horopito						•								•	•			•	
Ranunculus insignis	Korikori	yellow			•			•			•	•			•				•	
Ranunculus lyallii	Mt Cook lily	white			•				•		•	•			•				•	
Rhopalostylis sapida	Nikau	red					•					•			•	•			•	•
Rubus australis	Tataramoa, Bush lawyer	white				•					•				•	•			•	
Rubus schmidelioides	Bush lawyer	white				•					•				•	•			•	
Scandia rosifolia	Rose-leaved anise	white			•			•				•			•				•	
Selliera radicans		white			•			•				•	•		•			•	•	•
Senecio compactus		yellow					•					•			•			•	•	
Senecio elaeagnifolius							•								•	•			•	
Senecio greyi		yellow					•					•			•				•	
Senecio hectori		white					•					•			•	•			•	
Senecio huntii	Rautini	yellow					•					•			•				•	
Senecio laxifolius		white					•					•			•				•	
Sonchus oleraceus	Puwha		•					•							•			•		

SCIENTIFIC NAME	COMMON NAME	COLOUR	PLANT TYPE					HEIGHT			SEASON				SUN			MOISTURE		
			Annual	Biennial	Perennial	Climber	Shrub/Tree	Under 30 cm	30–90 cm	Over 90 cm	Spring	Summer	Autumn	Winter	Full sun	Part sun	Shady	Dryish	Average	Wettish
Sophora microphylla	Kowhai	yellow					●				●				●				●	
Sophora tetraptera	Kowhai	yellow					●				●				●				●	
Tecomanthe speciosa		yellow				●							●	●	●				●	
Tetragonia tetragonioides	NZ spinach		●					●							●	●			●	
Tetrapathaea tetrandra	Kohia, NZ passion vine	white, orange berries				●					●		●		●	●			●	
Viola cunninghamii	NZ violet	white			●			●			●					●			●	
Wahlenbergia albomarginata	NZ harebell	white, blue			●			●				●			●				●	

COTTAGE
ROSES

With thousands of rose varieties to choose from, how do you decide what is best for your cottage garden? The following limited selection is intended to get you going: the roses on this list are not the only ones which will fit the relaxed cottage style of gardening, but they are roses which have given much satisfaction in the past. The list focuses on bush and climbing roses, most of them scented and a lot of them recurrent (more than one flowering). It is divided into 'Traditional', 'Old' and 'Modern' sections, by colour. Traditional roses are the ones known to the original cottagers, and although not as bright as modern varieties, they are rich in historical associations. The 'old' roses were mainly bred in the nineteenth century (a few go back to the eighteenth century and some come into the early twentieth century). The 'modern' roses given here may have been bred since the First World War, but they have been bred to suit the cottage style of garden. They are soft and delicate, not stiff and gaudy. For colour pictures of these roses, and more information about them, consult the rose books listed in the Bibliography. Rose gardens and nurseries which specialise in old roses are listed in Chapter 8, and a visit with a notebook in flowering season is the best way to find out what you really like.

NAME	COLOUR	SHAPE — Bush	SHAPE — Climber/Rambler
TRADITIONAL ROSES			
'Great Maiden's Blush'	white		●
Rosa alba semi-plena 'White Rose of York'	white	●	
R. damascena versicolor 'York and Lancaster'	white and pink	●	
R. gallica versicolor 'Rosa Mundi'	pink and white	●	
R. gallica offinalis 'Apothecary's Rose', 'Red Rose of Lancaster'	red	●	
R. spinosissima Scotch Briar	white, pink	●	
R. rugosa	white, red hips	●	
R. damascena triginitipetala 'Rose of Kazanlik'	pink	●	
'Ispahan'	pink	●	
OLD ROSES			
'Boule de Neige'	white	●	
'Madame Hardy'	white	●	
'Alberic Barbier'	creamy white		●
'Felicite et Perpetue'	white		●
'Blanc Double de Coubert'	white	●	
R. multiflora grandiflora	white		●
R. banksiae plena	white		●

NAME	COLOUR	SHAPE — Bush	SHAPE — Climber/Rambler
'Fantin Latour'	blush pink	●	
'Madame Pierre Oger'	blush pink	●	
'Baronne Prevost'	pink	●	
'Konigin von Danemark'	pink	●	
'La Reine Victoria'	pink	●	
'Souvenir de la Malmaison'	pale pink	●	
'Cecile Brunner' ('Sweetheart Rose')	pink	●	
'Variegata di Bologna'	pink and white	●	
R. mutabilis	orange-pink-red	●	●
'Charles de Mills'	mauve-red	●	
'Souvenir de Doctor Jamain'	wine red	●	
'Reine des Violettes'	violet-red	●	
'Madame Isaac Pereire'	purple-crimson	●	
'Robert le Diable'	crimson/lilac	●	
R. banksiae lutea	yellow		●
'Marechal Niel'	yellow	●	
'Crepuscule'	apricot		●
'Goldfinch'	yellow-cream		●

NAME	COLOUR	Bush	Climber/ Rambler	NAME	COLOUR	Bush	Climber/ Rambler
		SHAPE				**SHAPE**	
MODERN ROSES							
'Iceberg'	white	●		'Albertine'	pink		●
'Margaret Merrill'	pinkish-white	●		'New Dawn'	pink		●
'Nevada'	cream	●		'Nancy Steen'	cream/salmon pink	●	
'Sea Foam'	creamy-white		●	*R. moyesii*	red/red hips	●	
'Raubritter'	pink	●		'Paul's Scarlet'	scarlet		●
'Nozomi'	pale pink	●		'Graham Thomas'	yellow	●	
'The Fairy'	pink	●		'Golden Wings'	yellow		●

REFERENCES

Chapter 1

1 Morton, Elsie K., *Gardening's Such Fun!*, Unity Press Ltd, 1944, pp. 47–8.

2 Lakeman, Howard and Heber, in *Letters from Otago 1848–1849* Victorian New Zealand – A Reprint Series No. 4, Hocken Library, 1978, pp. 20–1.

3 Earp, G. B., *New Zealand: Its Emigration and Gold Fields*, quoted in Jeremy Salmon, *Old New Zealand Houses 1800–1940*, Reed Methuen, 1986, p. 63.

4 Courage, Sarah, *Lights and Shadows of Colonial Life*(1896), Whitcoulls, 1976, p. 18.

5 Jekyll, Gertrude, *On Gardening*, Introduction by Elizabeth Lawrence, Charles Scribner's Sons, 1964, p. 88.

6 *ibid*, p. 89.

7 Cutler, H. G., 'Beauty and Utility in the Home Garden', *The New Zealand Fruitgrower*, 17 March 1919, p. 269.

8 Walling, Edna, *Cottage and Garden in Australia*, Melbourne University Press, 1947, p. 111.

9 Sackville-West, Vita, *Vita Sackville-West's Garden Book*, ed. Philippa Nicolson, Michael Joseph, 1968, pp. 24–5.

10 Graham, Maire, 'A Granny's Garden', in *Dittany*, Vol. 8, New Zealand Herb Societies, 1987, pp. 30, 31.

Chapter 2

1 Scott-James, Anne and Lancaster, Osbert, Chapter One 'Roman Britain' in *The Pleasure Garden*, John Murray, 1977.

2 Information in this chapter on which plants were introduced and when they were grown is taken from Fisher, John, *The Origins of Garden Plants*, Constable, 1982, and Fleming, Lawrence, and Gore, Alan, *The English Garden*, Michael Joseph, 1979. Additional information on English garden history is from Fleming and Gore and Scott-James and Lancaster.

3 For a little more detail on plants grown in Britain between AD 500 and 900, see Webb, Anne, 'Of Wild Herbs, Weeds and Worts', *New Zealand Gardener*, Vol. 45, Issue 4, April 1989, pp. 54–5.

4 Cooper Kelley Palmer, Mary, *The Early English Kitchen Garden: Medieval Period to AD 1800*, Trinity Press, 1984.

5 Scott-James and Lancaster, *op. cit.*, Chapter Three, 'The Pleasaunce'.

6 Genders, Roy, 'The English Cottage Garden Through the Ages' in *The Cottage Garden and the Old-fashioned Flowers*, Pelham Books, 1969.

7 Information on the eighteenth- and nineteenth-century English cottage garden taken from Scott-James, Anne, *The Cottage Garden*, Penguin Books, 1982.

Chapter 3

1 Scott-James, Anne, *The Cottage Garden*, Penguin Books, 1982, pp. 54–5.

2 Arnold, Rollo, *The Farthest Promised Land*, Victoria University Press, 1981, p. 191.

3 *ibid*, p. 158.

4 Leach, Helen, *1,000 Years of Gardening in New Zealand*, Reed, 1984, p. 111.

5 *ibid*, pp. 111–13.

6 Drummond, Alison, *Married and Gone to New Zealand*, Pauls Book Arcade, 1960, p. 78.

7 Godley, Charlotte, *Letters from Early New Zealand 1850–1853*, Whitcombe and Tombs, 1951, p. 31.

8 *ibid*, p. 85.

9 *ibid*, p. 133.

10 *ibid*, p. 141.

11 Maling, Peter Bromley, *Samuel Butler at Mesopotamia*, Government Printer, 1960, pp. 25–6.

12 Hale, Allen, *Pioneer Nurserymen of New Zealand*, A. H. & A. W. Reed, 1955, p. 40.

13 *ibid*, p. 41.

14 Lawrence, Jean, *Gardens Full of Wings*, Millwood, 1976, p. 12.

15 Pillans, F. S., *Diary 1 January 1850–2 June 1852*, Manuscript, Otago Early Settlers Museum, p. 6.

16 *ibid*, p. 26.

17 *ibid* (25 December 1850).

18 Menzies, Dr J. A. R., *Diary 1853–1857*, Manuscript, Otago Early Settlers Museum, p. 4.

19 Dawber, Robert, *Diary November 1, 1868–December 14, 1869*, Manuscript, Canterbury Museum (8.1.1869).

20 *ibid*, (2.3.1869).

21 *ibid*, (3.3.1869).

22 McClinton, Mrs, *Early Memories of Cust and Leithfield*, Manuscript, Canterbury Museum, p. 4.

23 *Chapman's Settlers Handbook to the Farm and Garden*, G. T. Chapman [1873], p. 89.

24 Murphy, M., *Handbook of Gardening for New Zealand*, Whitcombe and Tombs [1885], Preface.

25 Anonymous, 'Cottage Gardening', *Bond's Waikato Almanac*, 1892, pp. 105–9.

26 Cutler, H. G., 'Beauty and Utility in the Home Garden', *The New Zealand Fruitgrower*, 17 March 1919, p. 269.

27 Young, James and Hay, D., *Flower Gardening in New Zealand*, Whitcombe and Tombs [1919?], p. 12.

28 *ibid*, p. 13.

29 *ibid*, p. 7.

30 *ibid*, p. 13.

31 *ibid*, pp. 57–8.

32 *ibid*, p. 27.

33 Dann, Christine, *Leonard Cockayne – A Biographical Sketch*, unpublished manuscript, 1986, p. 5. All quotes from Cockayne taken from his manuscript 'The Little Boy and the English Wood' (1934) in the National Museum.

34 *ibid*, p. 8.

35 'Competition for Gardens. Beautifying Association's Work', newspaper clipping in Vol. 2 of the Minute Book of the Christchurch Beautifying Association (1930s), p. 194 (Canterbury Museum). The actual quote, from Mr Irving Sladen, donor of the cup for the winner of the Beautifying Association's garden competition, was: 'The man with the garden that all could see as they went by was showing a higher form of citizenship.'

36 Morton, Elsie K., *Gardening's Such Fun!*, Unity Press, 1944, pp. 53–4.

Chapter 4

1 Isdale, A. M., 'Experiences with Herbs' in *Dittany* No. 1, 1979, p. 18.

Chapter 5

1 Robinson, William, *The English Flower Garden*, The Amaryllis Press, 1984 (facsimile of 15th edition), p. 32.

2 Strong, Roy, *Creating Small Gardens*, Conran Octopus, 1986, p. 7.

Chapter 6

1 Plumb, Vivienne, 'Borage Led the Way' in *Dittany* No. 6, 1984, pp. 14–15.

Chapter 7

1 Genders, Roy, *The Cottage Garden and the Old-fashioned Flowers*, Pelham Books, 1983, p. 9.

Chapter 8

1 Leach, Helen, *1,000 Years of Gardening in New Zealand*, Reed, 1984, pp. 122–3.

BIBLIOGRAPHY

The cottage tradition

Cooper Kelley Palmer, Mary, *The Early English Kitchen Garden*, Trinity Press, 1983.

Cuffley, Peter, *Cottage Gardens in Australia*, The Five Mile Press, 1983.

Genders, Roy, *The Cottage Garden and the Old-fashioned Flowers*, Pelham Books, 1983 (1969).

Genders, Roy, *The Cottage Garden Year*, Croom Helm, 1986.

Hyams, Edward, *English Cottage Gardens*, Whittet Books, 1986 (1970).

Scott-James, Anne, *The Cottage Garden*, Penguin Books, 1982.

Swindells, Philip, *Cottage Gardening in Town and Country*, Ward Lock Ltd, 1986.

Thompson, Flora, *Lark Rise to Candleford, A Trilogy*, Penguin 1983, and *The Illustrated Lark Rise to Candleford*, abridged by Julian Shuckburgh, Cantury Publishing Co., 1983. (A contemporary account of cottage and village life in nineteenth-century Britain.)

Whiten, Faith and Geoff, *Making a Cottage Garden*, Unwin Hyman, 1986.

Garden design

Bartholomew, Mel, *Square Foot Gardening*, Rodale Press, 1981. (Organic potager-style vegetable gardening for small spaces.)

Berrisford, Judith, *The Very Small Garden Unlimited Ideas for Limited Space*, Faber and Faber, 1968.

Carman, Kerry, *The Creative Gardener*, Reed Methuen, 1987. (Best New Zealand advice from a gardener who knows how to turn the romance of cottage gardening into reality.)

Clark, Ethne and Perry, Clay, *English Country Gardens*, Weidenfeld and Nicolson, 1985.

Cooper, Guy and Taylor, Gordon, *English Herb Gardens*, Weidenfeld and Nicolson, 1986.

Dixon, Trisha and Churchill, Jennie, *Gardens in Time. In the Footsteps of Edna Walling*, Angus and Robertson, 1988. (A full-colour introduction to the inspired gardens of this great Australian designer.)

Hobhouse, Penelope, *Colour in Your Garden*, Collins, 1984. (English but inspirational.)

Hobhouse, Penelope, *Garden Style*, Georgian House (Melbourne), 1988.

Jekyll, Gertrude, *On Gardening*, Introduction by Elizabeth Lawrence, Charles Scribner's Sons, 1964.

Jekyll, Gertrude, *Gertrude Jekyll on Gardening*, edited with a commentary by Penelope Hobhouse, Macmillan, 1983.

Lacey, Stephen, *The Startling Jungle. Colour and Scent in the Romantic Garden*, Viking, 1986.

Page, Russell, *The Education of a Gardener*, Penguin Books, 1985 (1962).

Sackville-West, Vita, *The Illustrated Garden Book*, a new anthology by Robin Lane Fox, Macdonald Orbis, 1988.

Scott-James, Anne, *Sissinghurst. The Making of a Garden*, Michael Joseph, 1975.

Scott-James, Anne and Lancaster, Osbert, *The Pleasure Garden*, Penguin Books, 1979 (1977).

Strong, Roy, *Creating Small Gardens*, Conran Octopus, 1986. (A book of above-average ideas for people with average incomes.)

Cottage plants and planting

Chambers, John, *Wild Flower Garden*, Elm Tree Books, 1987.

Chatto, Beth, *The Damp Garden*, Dent, 1982.

Chatto, Beth, *The Dry Garden*, J. M. Dent & Sons, 1981.

Coats, Alice, *Flowers and their Histories*, Adam and Charles Black, 1956.

Dunn, Olive, *Delights of a Fragrant Garden in New Zealand*, Century Hutchinson, 1989.

Fish, Margery, *Cottage Garden Flowers*, Faber and Faber, 1980 (1960).

Fisher, John, *The Origins of Garden Plants*, Constable, 1982.

Lane Fox, Robin, *Better Gardening*, R. and L., 1982. (Great hints on the best varieties of trees, shrubs, border plants and bulbs.)

Genders, Roy, *The Cottage Garden and the Old-fashioned Flowers*, Pelham Books, 1969.

Gordon, Lesley, *Poorman's Nosegay: Flowers from a Cottage Garden*, Collins Harvill Press, 1973.

Griffiths, Trevor, *My World of Old Roses*, Whitcoulls, 1987 (1983).

Keen, Mary, *The Garden Border Book*, Viking, 1987.

Kelly, Frances, *A Perfumed Garden*, Methuen Australia, 1981.

Lloyd, Christopher, *The Adventurous Gardener*, Allen Lane, 1983.

Lloyd, Christopher, *The Well-tempered Garden*, Collins, 1971.

New Zealand Herb Societies, *Dittany*, annual journal of New Zealand Herb Societies, Herb Foundation of New Zealand Inc., P.O. Box 20-022, Glen Eden, Auckland.

Sackville-West, Vita, *Vita Sackville-West's Garden Book*, edited by Philippa Nicolson, Michael Joseph, 1968.

Steen, Nancy, *The Charm of Old Roses*, Reed Methuen, 1987 (1966). (This book and Trevor Griffiths' book are by New Zealanders, and describe what is available here.)

Painter, Gilian and Power, Elaine, *The Herb Garden Displayed*, Hodder and Stoughton, 1978.

Painter, Gilian and Power, Elaine, *A Garden of Old Fashioned and Unusual Herbs*, Hodder and Stoughton, 1982.

Robinson, William, *The English Flower Garden*, The Amaryllis Press, 1984 (facsimile of 15th edition, 1933).

Verey, Rosemary, *The Scented Garden*, Michael Joseph, 1981.

New Zealand gardens, cottages and plants

Brooker, S. G., Cambie, R. C. and Cooper, R. C., *New Zealand Medicinal Plants*, Heinemann, 1981.

Budden, H., *Bulbous Flowers: A Colonial Nurseryman's Catalogue*, Oxford University Press, 1979. (Colour facsimiles from Budden's nineteenth-century catalogue, with additional information.)

Carman, Kerry, *Portrait of a Garden*, Reed, 1983.

Cartman, Joe, *Growing New Zealand Alpine Plants*, Reed Methuen, 1985.

Fisher, Muriel, Satchell, E., and Watkins, Janet, *Gardening with New Zealand Plants, Shrubs and Trees*, Collins, 1985.

Hale, Allen, *Pioneer Nurserymen of New Zealand*, A. H. & A. W. Reed, 1955.

Lawrence, Jean, *Gardens Full of Wings: Notes of a Wilderness Gardener*, Millwood Press, 1976.

Lawrence, Jean, *Gardening Tales*, Millwood Press, 1981.

Leach, Helen, *1,000 Years of Gardening in New Zealand*, Reed, 1984.

MacDonald, Christina, *Medicines of the Maori*, Collins, 1974.

Matthews, Barbara, *Gardens of New Zealand*, Lansdowne Press, 1983.

Matthews, Julian, *New Zealand Native Plants for Your Garden*, Pacific Publishers, 1987.

Metcalf, L. J., *The Cultivation of New Zealand Trees and Shrubs*, Reed Methuen, 1987.

Morton, Elsie K., *Gardening's Such Fun!*, Unity Press, 1944.

Salmon, J. T., *New Zealand Flowers and Plants in Colour*, Reed, 1970 (1963).

Salmond, Jeremy, *Old New Zealand Houses 1800–1940*, Heinemann Reed, 1986.

Organic gardening

French, Jackie, *The Organic Garden Doctor*, Angus & Robertson, 1988.

Hudson, Richard Llewellyn, *Organic Gardening in New Zealand*, Reed, 1982.

Seymour, John, *The Self-sufficient Gardener*, Oxford University Press (Australian and New Zealand edition), 1978. (Good general gardening manual, plus chapter on preserving produce.)

Soil and Health Association of New Zealand, *Soil and Health* (quarterly), Box 2824, Auckland.

Strickland, Sue, *Planning the Organic Flower Garden*, Thorsons, 1986.

My most-used manuals

Bremness, Lesley, *The Complete Book of Herbs. A practical guide to growing and using herbs*, R.D. Press, 1988. (Beautifully designed but also very practical.)

Crooks, Michael, *The New Zealand Gardening Calendar A Month-by-Month Guide*, Reed Methuen, 1981.

Ferguson, Nicola, *Right Plant, Right Place*, Pan Books, 1984. (Invaluable full-colour reference to which plants to plant where.)

Hale, Beatrice and Hinds, Elizabeth, *The New Zealand Herb Calendar. A Season-by-Season Guide*, Reed Methuen, 1986.

Mitchell, Susanne and Haynes, Barbara (eds), *The Hamlyn Guide to Plant Propagation*, Hamlyn, 1982.

Perry, Frances (ed.), *The Macdonald Encyclopedia of Plants & Flowers*, Macdonald, 1980.

Toogood, Alan, *The Planter's Encyclopedia of Perennials*, Macdonald Orbis, 1988.

Miscellaneous

Browne, Mary, Leach, Helen and Tichbourne, Nancy, *The Cook's Garden. For Cooks who Garden and Gardeners who Cook*, A. H. & A. W. Reed, 1980.

Browne, Mary, Leach, Helen and Tichbourne, Nancy, *More From the Cook's Garden*, Reed Methuen, 1987. (Invaluable New Zealand advice.)

Fox, Matthew, *Original Blessing. A Primer in Creation Spirituality*, Bear and Company, 1983. (Appropriate spirituality for cottage gardening.)

McIlraith, Isabel, *Tussies Mussies, or Victorian Posies from my Cottage Garden on a Steep Hillside*, Black Robin, 1983. (If you can produce these quaint posies in Wellington you can produce them anywhere.)

Milo Ohrbach, Barbara, *The Scented Room*, Doubleday, 1986. (Indoor fragrance from flowers and flower preparations.)

Polson, Gillian, *The Living Kitchen: A New Zealand Companion to Herbs, Wholefoods, Health and Happiness*, Benton Ross, 1983.

INDEX

Page numbers in *italics* indicate illustrations